The Laurel Brigade at Brandy Station:
A Military Staff Ride

Written by

Master Sergeant Phillip R. Gibbons, USMC (Ret)

Edited by

Major Bruce H. "Doc" Norton, USMC (Ret)

The Laurel Brigade at Brandy Station:
A Military Staff Ride

Written by

Master Sergeant Phillip R. Gibbons, USMC (Ret)

Edited by

Major Bruce H. "Doc" Norton, USMC (Ret)

Academica Press
Washington~London

This book is dedicated to those
who made the ultimate sacrifice
in the defense of their nation
on the fields of Brandy Station.

Library of Congress Cataloging-in-Publication Data
Names: Gibbons, Phillip R. (author) | Norton, Bruce H. (editor)
Title: The laurel brigade at brandy station : a military staff ride | Phillip R. Gibbons | Bruce H. Norton
Description: Washington : Academica Press, 2024. | Includes references.
Identifiers: LCCN 2023949557 | ISBN 9781680535549 (hardcover) | 9781680532630 (paperback) | 9781680535556 (e-book)

Copyright 2024 Phillip R. Gibbons

Unknown Confederate Grave
Warrenton Cemetery, Warrenton, VA

Acknowledgments

I want to thank all of those who contributed to the research and writing of this book: The Marshall, Stribling, and Massie families for sharing so many stories of their ancestors who served in the Laurel Brigade. Fellow Marine Clark "Bud" Hall for the wonderful work he has done at the Brandy Station Battlefield, and for sharing his research through staff rides and conversations. Joseph McKinney, the former President of the Brandy Station Foundation, with whom I spent numerous hours on the Brandy Station battlefield, some of which were on horseback, while discussing the battle in great detail. He kindly answered my numerous questions and provided clarity and an officer's perspective. My fellow cavalry historian Captain Brian Petruskie, DVM and President of the Eastern Seaboard Cavalry Association, Dr. Bruce Gudmundsson, Tom Bookwalter, Ron Bingham, and Bob O'Neill. All the troopers who kindly allowed me to ride alongside of them, particularly, John Perry and the troopers of the 2nd U.S. Dragoons (reenacted) and the 1st Virginia Cavalry (reenacted). The volunteers of the Brandy Station Foundation were so very kind to me during my research. My good friend and author Don Vandergrift provided context to the relevance of Mission Command. The excellent author and historian, Mr. Michael Block. A hearty thanks to the exceptionally talented author and Brandy Station historian Eric Wittenburg. A special thank you to Gunnery Sergeant Tom Williams and Bill Freuh who made riding the Brandy Station battlefield a special treat. To Colonel John Favors, the late Lieutenant Colonel David Stanley, and John Ruf for their expert instruction on horse artillery and projectiles. Troy Morton and Lisa Moore of Marine Corps University for mentorship and reviewing chapters of this handbook during their limited free time. The American Battlefield Trust, whose tireless efforts, with those of other organizations, have preserved the ground around Brandy Station, a place where Americans have fought and died and still to this day is the resting place for some of those soldiers as they still lay, buried where they fell. The late Don Warlick who led many a staff ride from horseback and provided expert horsemanship instruction. Dr. Paul du Quenoy, President and Publisher of Academica Press, believed in me to see this project through to the end. A HUGE thank you to my editor, military historian, mentor, and good friend, Major Bruce H. "Doc" Norton, USMC (ret). He kept me on task, reviewed chapters, spent time with me at Brandy Station, accompanied me while tramping through graveyards in search of headstones, and spent many hours with me driving all over the place while conducting research. Finally, I must mention my old warhorse and friend Garryowen. He carried me all over Brandy Station while doing research and never once complained. A huge thank you to my family – without their support, this handbook would not have been possible.

Phillip R. Gibbons

Author and Garryowen

Contents

Acknowledgments ix

Introduction 1

Chapter 1
The Origins of the Laurel Brigade 5

Chapter 2
Biographical sketches of the Brigades key leaders 21

Chapter 3
The March to Culpeper 37

Chapter 4
The Staff Ride 39
Stop 1A – Laurel Brigade Camp Dayton – Dove Park 39
Stop 1B – Laurel Brigade Camp near Elkton – 41
Stop 1C – Laurel Brigade Camp Green/Madison County Line – 42
Stop 1D – Laurel Brigade Camp Bethel Church
– near Madison, Virginia 44
Stop 1E – Laurel Brigade Camp east of Culpeper – Wine Street
Memorial Park 46
Stop 2 – The Grand Review 48
Stop 3 – Captain Gibson's Picket line – Near Beverly Ford 52
Stop 4 – Beckham's Artillery Battalion camp –
American Battlefield Trust parking lot 58
Stop 5 – Saint James Church – American Battlefield Trust parking lot .. 64
Stop 6 – Fleetwood Heights – American Battlefield Trust parking lot ... 69
Stop 7 – Graffiti House – Brandy Station Foundation parking lot 79
Summary 83

Chapter 5
Reflection 85
Brigade and Regimental Commanders 85
6th Virginia Cavalry 91
7th Virginia Cavalry 96
11th Virginia Cavalry 98
12th Virginia Cavalry 100
35th Battalion Virginia Cavalry 106
Chew's Battery 107

Appendix A 111

Appendix B 113

Appendix C 117

Appendix D 119

Appendix E 123

Appendix F 125

Appendix G 127

Appendix H 131

Appendix I 135

Appendix J 141

Endnotes 143

Select Bibliography 145
Books, Manuscripts and Manuals 145
Newspapers 147

Introduction

The intent of this book is to provide a user's guide for use on the Brandy Station Battlefield while touring the sites associated with the Laurel Brigade. Maps and photographs produced in chronological order will assist the users as they follow the line of march from the Shenandoah Valley through Culpeper County and across the field of Brandy Station with the most storied brigade of Confederate Cavalry. Photographs of key commanders, artifacts, and locations on the battlefield will bring the stories of these brave soldiers to life.

Why another book on Brandy Station? Excellent books have been written on the subject and cover the battle of Brandy Station in detail. They discuss actions at the strategic and operational levels. This staff ride handbook, however, is not about the entire battle, which spans a 10-mile square area, but rather a single brigade of soldiers, focusing on actions at the lowest level of war: the "tactical" level. The book will explore human-interest stories, relate personal accounts, and examine actions from the brigade level down to the individual cavalry trooper.

Some of the most contested ground from the battle is the most easily accessible to the public. This also happens to be the ground the Laurel Brigade camped and fought across in early June 1863. This book will take you to those locations through the staff ride process. For those unfamiliar with the military style of staff ride, it is a three-phase study. The first phase, preliminary, provides background information that the staff ride participant will need to not only understand the story being told, but to also provide information of the "5-Ws": Who, What, Where, When, and Why? The next phase is the staff ride itself, on the ground where the battle took place. Finally, a phase of reflection. Sometimes it is referred to as the "So what?" phase. Why does any of this matter? What are the lessons learned? How did the outcome shape and impact future actions? The "staff ride" traces its origins in the United States Military to the early

1900s, with the Army's Command and General Staff College. Since that time, the staff ride has undergone numerous changes and is now a key tool for educating our nation's military leaders at every level of professional military education for both officers and enlisted men and women.

If you want to have a good time, jine the cavalry!
Jine the cavalry! Jine the cavalry!
If you want to catch the Devil, if you want to have fun,
If you want to smell Hell, jine the cavalry!

Sam Sweeney

Chapter 1

The Origins of the Laurel Brigade

Those of us who study mounted operations during the American Civil War are not strangers to hearing the exploits of the famous "Laurel Brigade" – stories of Ashby's Cavalry and Stonewall Jackson's Infantry fighting the "Yankees" in the Shenandoah Valley.

The units of the Laurel Brigade that participated in the fighting at Brandy Station varied from pre-war militia companies to units of volunteers answering the call to arms. A few of the companies had origins going back to the War of 1812, and a couple were even older. The troopers varied from those with professional training at a military academy to unskilled laborers with no formalized training prior to enlisting. These troopers were mostly from central and western counties of Virginia. Some joined up as individuals, others enlisted together with brothers and cousins, or as fathers and sons. The troopers all answered the call when the time came to defend their homes.

The Sixth Virginia Cavalry was formed from individual companies mustering at a camp of instruction in Ashland, Virginia, under Charles William Field, who was a commissioned a Confederate colonel. Field was a native of Kentucky and until recently had served as a cavalry officer in the 2nd U.S. Cavalry. Following some shuffling of companies, and after a few months had passed, the regiment was organized as follows:

Dulany Troop, Company A
Rappahannock Cavalry/The Old Guard, Company B
Rockingham Boys, Company C
Clarke Cavalry, Company D
Georgia Hussars, Company E – transferred to Jeff Davis Legion 7 Dec 1861

Fairfax Cavalry, Company F
Flournoy Troop, Company G
Wise Dragoons, Company H
Orange Rangers, Company I
Loudon Cavalry, Company K

The regiment would maintain this organization until Colonel Fields's promotion to Brigadier General on 27 March 1862. On 15 April, three new field officers would be assigned to the regiment: Colonel Julien Harrison, Lieutenant Colonel J. Grattan Caball, and Major Thomas Stanhope Flournoy. These assignments would be short-lived due to the nature of the Conscription Act passed by the Confederate Congress.[1] This act permitted units to elect their own officers. As one can imagine, this resulted in more than a few changes in leadership at both company and regimental levels. The company officers, including twenty newly elected ones, then set about selecting field officers. Julien Harrison would remain as Colonel of the regiment. Thomas Stanhope Flournoy would be elevated from Major to the Lieutenant Colonel billet. Former company officer John Shackelford "Shac" Green was elected as Major of the regiment. This left J. Grattan Caball without a job.

Also in April, another company was assigned to the regiment, likely to replace the missing Georgians of Company E, who had transferred out months earlier. The Pittsylvania Dragoons, led by Captain Cabell Flournoy, were a seasoned company who had performed well in several engagements. This assignment was the result of efforts by the 6th's Lieutenant Colonel, Thomas Stanhope Flournoy, who was also Captain Cabell Flournoy's father. Of note, Cabell's brother Henry was serving in Company G, and later as an orderly to their father.[2]

The Sixth Virginia would spend the early summer of 1862 operating alongside the Second Virginia Cavalry and being assigned to Lieutenant General Richard S. Ewell's Division for operations in the Shenandoah Valley. In July, there would be more reorganization for the Sixth. They were assigned to a brigade of cavalry led by Beverly Robertson being formed just outside of Richmond. The new brigade would consist of the 2nd, 6th, 7th, and 12th Regiments of cavalry along with the 17th Battalion of Virginia Cavalry. There were also leadership changes for the

Sixth as well. Colonel Harrison resigned due to a case of severe and chronic hemorrhoids. Thomas Flournoy took over with a promotion to Colonel, and Cabell Flournoy was elected Major, with "Shac" Green becoming Lieutenant Colonel.

In mid-August, the cavalry operating under Jackson in the Valley was assigned to General J.E.B. Stuart's Cavalry Division in the Army of Northern Virginia. Robertson would be at the front of the brigade until 5 September, when he was assigned to training new cavalry in North Carolina.[3] Colonel Thomas Munford of the 2nd Virginia Cavalry was appointed to lead the brigade. Munford would retain leadership of the brigade until 8 November, when Brigadier General William E. "Grumble" Jones was appointed to command. Munford reverted to commanding the 2nd Virginia Cavalry, and both he and the regiment were transferred to Fitzhugh Lee's brigade. It is at this point that we see the placement of the 6th Virginia into the brigade as structured for campaigning of 1863. Jones's brigade consisted of the 6th, 7th, and 12th Regiments of Virginia Cavalry. Also, two battalions of cavalry were assigned, the 17th and 35th. In January, the 17th Battalion was elevated to regimental size and renamed the 11th Regiment of Virginia Cavalry.

In late September of 1862, the Regimental leadership suffered casualties both in and out of combat. Colonel Flournoy took sick leave on 20 September, leaving "Shac" Green to command the regiment. Green was wounded two days later near Paris, Virginia, receiving multiple saber wounds to the head, and subsequently captured by the Union Army. Command thus fell on the shoulders of 22-year-old Major Cabell Flournoy. Although his father, Colonel Stanhope Flournoy, would remain on the rolls in leave status, his son Cabell would lead the regiment in the field for the remainder of 1862 and throughout the following year. Julien Harrison was re-commissioned as Colonel on 23 September 1862, having healed from his hemorrhoids, but for whatever reason, did not assume operational command. Perhaps he had not fully recovered?

Again, in December 1862, Harrison petitioned the Confederate Secretary of War for reinstatement as Colonel of the Sixth Virginia. But the question of being fit for field service was still a question to be answered. The second hurdle for Harrison was that the Sixth had been reorganized for the war. Officer promotions occurred by grade and seniority. All officers of the regiment would have to agree to being passed over in order for Harrison to reassume command.

In January 1863, the paroled and recovered "Shac" Green returned to duty with the Sixth Virginia and reassumed command. Although a lieutenant colonel by rank, he would fill the role of Regimental Colonel. Overall, an unfortunate theme developed of revolving field-grade officers to command the regiment, each with different philosophies and battlefield leadership styles, although there was at least the consistency with Major Cabell Flournoy, who had been in some form of regimental leadership since July.

The lack of permanent leadership in the regiment must have also caught the brigade commander's attention as Jones wrote to Robert E. Lee's headquarters on the matter in a letter dated 1 April 1863. Jones noted that Green, Flournoy, and Captain John Throckmorton, were all, by seniority, entitled to promotion and would thus bring the matter to a close. Later that month Jones's boss, J. E. B. Stuart, also commented on the bad condition of the regiment to Lee, but did not concur with Jones's recommendations for promotions. He preferred Charles W. Field to command the regiment. Lee agreed with Jones's recommendations as the men were "legally entitled" and Stuart's recommendations could only be adopted if Green was brought before a board and disqualified. With the matter unsettled, and complicated by the poor performance of the Sixth during a recent raid into West Virginia, Jones ordered the convening of a board of officers to determine if the current regimental officers were qualified to lead the regiment.

The board convened in late May 1863 and discussed the matter over a three-day period. On the 29th, the board announced the following: For the colonelcy of the regiment, Julian Harrison should be reappointed to command the Sixth. If Harrison were unable to take command due to policy or other, "Shac" Green should be appointed colonel. The board did not show well for Cabell Flournoy at all, recommending that he be relieved of all duties from the regiment.[4] The young Flournoy was described by Luther W. Hopkins of the Sixth, "A gallant young officer, but a little too fond of the bottle, not very choice in his language, rather reckless."[5] This lifestyle did not please Flounoy's fellow officers who were on the board. The eight officers who testified, including Green, found Flournoy "failing when it came to enforcing discipline and interior police, and in looking after the want of the men."[6] The outcome of the board would have to wait, as the entire Laurel Brigade had been ordered back east of the Blue Ridge to join Stuart at Culpeper.

The Seventh Virginia Cavalry can be said to have been the origin of the Laurel Brigade. Turner Ashby and his company of Mountain Rangers, of Fauquier County, Virginia, formed the nucleus of what would be a regiment and finally a brigade.[7] A West Point graduate and a man of 62 years of age, Colonel Angus W. McDonald would have Ashby's company assigned to him at Harpers Ferry. The company was assigned multiple missions as detachments and operated as scouts for the Army along the border. McDonald was flooded with requests from new troops to join his command, resulting in him gaining permission from the government to raise an independent regiment for border service.[8] McDonald would be the Colonel of the regiment, with Turner Ashby as Lieutenant Colonel and Oliver M. Funsten as Major.

On 17 June 1861, the regiment was organized into the following companies:

Fauquier County, Company A
Rockingham County, Company B
Shenandoah County, Company C
Page County, Company D
Warren County, Company E
Hampshire County, Company F
Maryland, Company G
Shenandoah County, Company H
Rockingham County, Company I
Shenandoah County, Company K

The companies of Robert Baylor and John Henderson would be added in September of 1861.[9]

The Seventh would be headquartered out of Romney and operate along the main line of communications of the Baltimore and Ohio Railroad. The regiment would serve in this initial capacity as cavalry for

Jackson's command, with the area of operations extending all the way to the headwaters of the Potomac. The Seventh would see action at Kelly's Island, Winchester, Manassas, Charlestown, Bolivar Heights, and hard fighting in and around the Romney area that led to Jackson's command being forced out.

Leadership of the Seventh would change in November with Col. McDonald's request to be relieved from command. Six months of strenuous duty in the saddle had taken its toll on the now 63-year-old McDonald. That, combined with the feeling of responsibility for the loss of Romney, McDonald asked to be relieved of command. Jackson obliged and transferred the colonel to the defenses of Winchester. Lt. Colonel Turner Ashby would assume command of the Seventh, much to the delight of many a trooper. He had proven himself as a leader on the battlefield and had the confidence of the men. On 12 February 1862, Ashby would receive a promotion to colonel securing his leadership of the Seventh.

Ashby proved to be an ideal leader in the eyes of his men. As word spread of Ashby's gallant cavalry, so did enlistments, swelling the ranks to 17 companies. Ashby's cavalry would see much field service with Stonewall Jackson's command in the Valley during the first quarter of 1862. The 7th Virginia would fight engagements at Kernstown, McDowell, Winchester, Strasburg, and all along the Valley Pike. By late April, Ashby was reporting a total of 23 companies of cavalry and a battery of artillery, more than double the original strength of the Seventh when formed eleven months earlier. The month of May would bring more fighting at Front Royal, Middletown, Cedarville, and Buckton Station. The string of victories brought with it a promotion for Ashby. On 27 May 1862, he was promoted to Brigadier General with an effective date of 23 May. Ashby's battlefield success, however, would end on the morning of 6 June near Port Republic. During rear guard action, while leading a charge on foot due to the loss of his horse in combat, he was shot through the heart, dying instantly. His last words were "Charge men … for God's sake, charge!"[10] Temporary command of Ashby's Valley Cavalry would fall to Colonel Thomas Munford the following day. General Lee wrote to the Secretary of War on Ashby's death "I grieve at the death of General Ashby, I hope he [Jackson] will find a successor."[11]

On 16 June 1862, the Seventh Virginia Cavalry was reorganized. Its 26 companies would be split into four separate units, with one company being transferred. The Seventh was reduced to 10 companies and was called the 1st Regiment of Ashby's cavalry. Another ten companies formed the 12th Virginia Cavalry, which was called the 2nd Regiment of Ashby's Cavalry. Five companies constituted the 17th battalion of Virginia Cavalry, which later became the 11th Virginia Cavalry. The one remaining company, commanded by Captain W. R. Preston, was transferred to the 14th Virginia Cavalry. The officers of the command met twice to select officers, per regulations, but their recommendations failed to meet War Department approval. On 18 June, Brigadier Beverly Robertson assumed command of the brigade of Valley Cavalry and made recommendations for officers. Colonel William E. Jones was selected as colonel, Captain R. H. Dulany was selected as Lieutenant Colonel, and Captain Thomas Marshall was made Major of the Seventh.

The remainder of the summer would see the Seventh in the field and involved in much action including Second Manassas and Sharpsburg. In one action near Orange Court House, Virginia, Major Marshall would personally be involved in severe hand to hand combat. This action bears witness to the lead from the front style of leadership that continued after Ashby's death:

> Major Marshall, being poorly mounted, fell behind and was soon surrounded by the enemy. His pistols empty, he drew his saber and tried to fight his way out. Cutting a path through the Federals, Marshall spurred his horse toward safety. Looking back over his shoulder to see if he was going to make it, the major detected the flash of a saber being swung at him. Throwing up his own saber too late to ward off the blow, Marshall was knocked senseless and captured. Colonel Jones came up in time to kill a federal trooper who was about to kill the wounded major. The enemy was too strong, and Jones had to leave Marshall behind.[12]

On 3 October Colonel Jones was promoted to Brigadier General. His vacancy as regimental colonel was filled by promoting Lieutenant Colonel Delany to the billet. Major Marshall was promoted to Lieutenant Colonel. Captain Samuel Myers was promoted to the Major billet. Just over a month later, General William Jones was assigned to command Roberton's, formerly Ashby's, brigade of cavalry. Jones' Brigade would consist of: The 6th, 7th, and 12th Regiments of Virginia Cavalry as well as the 17th (later the 11th Virginia Regiment), and the 35th Battalion of Virginia Cavalry. This is the first real organization of the brigade that would fight at Brandy Station the following year. The remainder of 1862 was spent drilling, conducting reconnaissance and picket duty, and practicing a regime of increased discipline under Jones's watchful eyes.

The year 1863 began with the Seventh continuing to train and conducting raids along with Jones' Brigade. They operated all along the Valley, including at Middletown, New Market, Winchester, Strasburg, and Woodstock. These types of operations would continue until mid-April, when Jones's Brigade teamed up with the forces of Brigadier General John D. Imboden to conduct joint raids into Maryland and western Virginia. The purpose of these raids was to disable the Baltimore and Ohio Railroad, defeat the Federal garrisons in the area, enlist fresh recruits into southern cavalry, and remove the pro-Union local government in the western part of Virginia. The Seventh would have about 500 troopers assigned to the 4,000-man combined task force. These operations continued until 12 May with varied success. Jones's Brigade then moved back to the vicinity of Dayton, Virginia, to rest and resupply and remained there until summoned to join Stuart's Cavalry Division at Brandy Station.

The Eleventh Virginia Cavalry was not formed officially until February 1863. The Eleventh's origins start with troopers of the Seventh Virginia Cavalry serving under Colonel McDonald and later General Ashby. Following the death of General Ashby, the massive, 26-company 7th Virginia Cavalry was broken up to form new regiments and battalions. Five companies formed the 17th Battalion of Virginia Cavalry with Major William Patrick in command. This unit would later form companies A to E of the Eleventh. Two additional companies would be assigned to the 17th Battalion in July 1862: Captain McChesney and Captain Daingerfield's companies, both from Bath County. These companies would be designated companies F and G. In early January 1863, Captain A. M. Pierce and his C company of the 24th Battalion of Virginia Cavalry would be reassigned to the 17th, becoming company H of the Eleventh. On 5 February, Army Headquarters assigned two additional companies from the 5th Virginia Cavalry to the 17th Battalion, bringing its strength up to ten companies. This permitted the War Department to redesignate the 17th Battalion the 11th Virginia Cavalry. On 18 February, the official word was received from the War Department and Lunsford L. Lomax was appointed regimental colonel. O. R. Funsten Sr. was appointed lieutenant colonel. Lomax's appointment did not sit well with the officers of the new regiment, as they preferred Funston, who was the current commander of the 17th Battalion.[13]

The newly formed 11th Virginia Cavalry would be structured as follows:

    Wildcat Company, Berkley and Frederick Counties, Company A
    Hardy Rangers, Hardy County, Company B
    Brock Gap Rifles, Rockingham County, Company C
    Hampshire County, Company D
    Valley Mounted Riflemen, Shenandoah and Rockbridge Counties, Company E
    Bath Greys, Bath and Pocahontas Counties, Company F
    Bath Guards, Bath and Highland Counties, Company G
    Frederick and Shenandoah Counties, Company H
    Fairfax Cavalry/Chesterfield Troop, Fairfax County, Company I
    Loudon, Clarke, and Gloucester Counties, Company K

Lt. Colonel Funsten continued to drill the new regiment while awaiting their new commander. The first major engagement for the 11th came on 26 February near Maurertown, the area between modern day Woodstock and Toms Brook, Virginia. Lt. Colonel Funsten's report to the brigade commander gives details of the action:

> The enemy was just beginning to retire, ignorant of our proximity, led by you (General Jones) we dashed past their rear guard, who occupied an eminence near the road and charged the rear of the column. So sudden and impetuous was the attack that every attempt made by their

officers to rally and form a line was unavailing. We pressed them hotly, using both saber and revolver with good effect, to Cedar Creek Bridge, about 12 miles, where a part of them made a stand.

The Eleventh would capture about 150 prisoners in the fight. The remainder of February and the month of March was spent on picket duty, drill, and acquiring replacement horses. From mid-April to 22 May, the Eleventh would take part in the previously mentioned Jones-Imboden Raids in western Virginia. The regiment performed well. Of note, Lt. Colonel Funsten did not participate in the raid and was left behind in charge of a rear detachment. These were men and horses who were not healthy enough to endure hardships of the raids into the western part of the state. Funsten's detachment did not sit idle, however, for it participated in two encounters near Fisher Hill and engaged in several other skirmishes.

In May, the 11th Virginia was sent to Strasburg for picket duty. They remained there until 3 June, when they return marched to Harrisonburg. Upon arrival, they continued toward Culpeper to rejoin the Laurel Brigade. The regiment linked up with Jones on the 7 June. With little rest, the 11th would take part in the grand review of cavalry the following day. Unlike the remainder of the brigade, the 11th would go into battle on the morning of 9 June with no time to rest or refit as the brigade had done at the camp in Dayton.

The Twelfth Regiment of Virginia Cavalry's origins resembled those of the 11th Virginia cavalry, as many of the troopers were originally part of the Seventh Virginia Cavalry serving under Colonel McDonald and, later, General Ashby. Ten companies out of 26 would be selected from 7th Virginia Cavalry to form the new 12th Virginia Cavalry. Colonel Asher Waterman Harmon was appointed to the colonelcy of the regiment with Richard Horseley Burks as the lieutenant colonel. Thomas Benjamin Massie was selected as regimental major.

The 12th Virginia Cavalry would be officially structured on 21 June 1862 as follows:

Jefferson County, Company A
Jefferson County, Company B
Frederick County, Company C

Jefferson County, Company D
Warren County, Company E
Various Counties, Company F
Rappahannock County, Company G
Rockingham County, Company H
Warren County, Company I
Shenandoah County, Company K

At the time of the 12th's organization, troop strength was 717 men based on official records analysis.[14]

The troopers of the 12th Regiment initial assignment was outpost duty in the Shenandoah Valley. Although assigned to Robertson's cavalry brigade, location separated the 12th from its brigade commander and thus Colonel Harmon acted independently of brigade orders. The regiment was quite successful in this capacity, gaining confidence and experience in both tactics and mounted skill at arms. Beginning on 1 August, the 12th would depart camp in Harrisonburg and report to Jackson's Army for duty minus two companies left behind to maintain eyes in the Valley under command of Thomas Massie. Reporting to their brigade commander, the 12th would now operate for the first time with the "Laurel Brigade" and Stuart's cavalry division.

On 20 August, the 12th engaged in combat with the brigade for the first time with excellent results. Stuart's division of cavalry was assigned to screen the advance of the Confederate infantry and to destroy the railroad bridge located at Rappahannock Station. Robertson's brigade, with the division commander attached, proceeded toward the area of Stevensburg. The Brigade contacted Federal Cavalry led by Brigadier George Bayard and the 12th and was ordered to charge the center of the Federal line with the remainder of the brigade in support of the charge. The weight of the 12th's charge proved too much for Bayard's troopers to withstand; they broke and withdrew to the cover of supporting artillery. The 12th and the whole brigade received plaudits from both Robertson and Stuart for "superior discipline, organization, and drill" in the day's action.

The 12th remained active for the remainder of the summer, participating in Stuart's ride around Pope's flank, the Second Battle of Manassas, and the Maryland Campaign. The continued operations had taken a toll on the 12th, with effective numbers being less than 100 troopers due to reassignments, combat losses, health issues, and broken-down mounts. The focus for the next two months would be on recruiting, refitting, and animal procurement, with picket duties added in. Operations for the remainder of the year remained quiet, outside an engagement in Berryville, with Brigadier General Jones now overseeing the brigade and General Robertson assigned to other duties. Following the recruiting period, the 12th moved into winter quarters with periodic offensive patrolling in the Valley. One might be critical of winter operations due to the harshness on both men and animals. But proficiency of both trooper and horse had to be maintained along with contact with the enemy so as not to lose situational awareness or initiative. Maintaining morale was even more important. Stagnation in winter camps combined with boredom was devastating for it. There would be none of that under the leadership of Jones in the Laurel Brigade.

The new year would see the 12th, along with the rest of the brigade, conducting operations all along the Valley through mid-April at which time the Laurel Brigade conducted joint raids into Maryland and western Virginia, under John Imboden's command. As noted, the purpose of these raids, which continued under 12 May, was to disable the Baltimore and Ohio Railroad, defeat the Federal garrisons in the area, enlist fresh recruits into southern cavalry and remove the pro-Union local government in the western part of Virginia. The brigade then moved back to Dayton, Virginia, for refit and supply. The 12th and the brigade remained there until departing to join Stuart's Cavalry Division at Brandy Station.

The 35th Battalion of Virginia Cavalry's organizational records begin on 11 January 1862. Its commander, Elijah Viers White, served briefly as a trooper in the 7th Virginia Cavalry before volunteering his services to Colonel Nathan Evans during the engagement at Balls Bluff. White served as a courier and scout for Evans's command and earned three commendations.[15] At Evans's insistence, White applied for a commission and was appointed captain in the Provisional Army. Captain White was authorized to raise an independent company for border warfare in the Virginia and Maryland area.

Records are scarce for the organization of the 35th Battalion. Early

January of 1862 is the first records in existence for "Whites Rebels."[16] Available records indicate the initial command was Captain Elijah V. White as battalion/company commander with an uncertain staff being assigned. Since White's command was initially only company strength, he used the company officers as staff. Of particular interest, many of the records related to recruiting indicate that the troopers enlisted "for war." On 19 March, the battalion command was organized with the following officers: 1st Lieutenant Frank M. Myers, 2nd Lieutenant William F. Barrett as recruiting officer, and 3rd Lieutenant R. C. Marlow as quartermaster.

Captain White's first assignment was to acquire wagons and teams. Immediately following this logistical assignment, the command was assigned scouting and observation duties near Waterford. This proved an ideal location for observation and scouting of Point of Rocks, Berlin, and nearby Harpers Ferry, by then occupied by a federal garrison. The company-sized command remained in this capacity at Waterford until early March, when the Confederate forces in the area were ordered to withdraw south. This presented a problem for White, for his command was formed for the purpose of border warfare. Withdrawing from the area took them away from nearby family and organized forces that could provide ordnance, medical, and quartermaster support. Nevertheless, White's small band of troopers moved south into Fauquier County along with the rest of the command.

While in Fauquier County, Captain White ran into Lt. Colonel Thomas Munford and two squadrons of the 2nd Virginia Cavalry. After some discussion, White's command attached itself to Munford's cavalry to assist with logistics and further organization along with guidance in conducting guerilla warfare. White's command remained under Munford through April, when they were assigned to General Richard S. Ewell's headquarters at Liberty Mills. The troopers served as couriers and scouts over the next several months for Ewell and the Valley Army.

White's command was formally organized as the 35th Battalion on 8 October 1862, having recruited the numbers needed for such a reorganization. White was elected major of the battalion with J. Mortimer Kilgour as quartermaster and 1st Lieutenant J. R. Brown appointed as adjutant. The companies were organized as follows:

Whites Rebels, Captain Frank Myers – Company A
Chiswell's Maryland Exiles, Captain George S. Chiswell – Company B
Captain R.B. Grubb – Company C
Captain James F. Trayhern, Maryland and Virginia troopers – Company D
Captain John H. Graybill, Page and Shenandoah Counties – Company E
Captain George N. Ferneyhough – Company F (organized later)

The new battalion spent late October and early November conducting small raids against detached units and Federal supply columns. In late November, the 35th was attached to General Jones Brigade headquarters and reported with orders to guard the Shenandoah River fords between Key's Ferry and Front Royal. This would permit Jones to screen all area crossing points from prying Federal eyes. The screening would result in a sharp engagement on 29 November, when Federal cavalry pushed across Castleman's Ferry, catching the defenders off-guard. This would result in a running fight all the way to Berryville, at which time the 12th Virginia Cavalry pitched into the fight offering a slight reprieve for the 35th. Outnumbered, the 35th and 12th withdrew to outside of Winchester, where the Federals decided to retire rather than continue the pursuit.

Major White took a slight thigh wound in this fight, his third wound of the war. For the remainder of the year, the 35th conducted a few successful raids into Federal-occupied territory, carrying off spoils of war to resupply their own. In late December, the 35th reported to the command of Brigadier General Jones's "Laurel" Cavalry Brigade. The days of being an independent command for the 35th were now over.

The new command structure did not sit well with the horse soldiers, resulting in many disgruntled troopers. The 35th spent the month of January drilling and acquiring the discipline and organization that Jones desired. To aid in this, Lieutenant Richard T. Watts of the 2nd Virginia Cavalry was appointed battalion adjutant. Other changes included Major White's promotion to lieutenant colonel and Captain Frank Myers's promotion to major. Sergeant John J. White was promoted to captain and made the new quartermaster. The following two months were spent in camp with continued drilling and reorganization. Despite this painful process, the 35th was improving in all areas, much to the pleasure of General Jones.

On 20 April, orders came to prepare for raid operations into western Virginia. The Laurel Brigade task force numbered close to 4,000 effectives with the added attachments and stepped off on 21 April. Its mission was to disable the Baltimore and Ohio Railroad, defeat the Federal garrisons in the area, enlist fresh recruits into southern cavalry and remove the pro-Union local government in the western part of Virginia. The 35th performed well over the next month, continuing to gain experience and confidence. The command returned to the Mount Crawford area, going into camp on 21 May. The 35th would have only nine days of rest and recuperation before stepping off with the brigade to join Stuart's Division at Brandy Station.

Chapter 2

Biographical sketches of the Brigades key leaders

The Laurel Brigade consisted of the 6th, 7th, 11th, 12th regiments of Virginia Cavalry, the 35th Battalion of Virginia Cavalry, and Chew's Battery of Artillery was attached for the march in from the Valley. The brigade was led by Brigadier General William E. Jones.

**Brigadier General William Edmondson "Grumble" Jones
Commanding Laurel Brigade**

Jones was born near Glade Spring, Washington County, Virginia, in May 1824. He attended Emory and Henry College prior to entering West Point, graduating in 1848. Jones received a commission as a brevet second lieutenant in the Regiment of Mounted Rifles and served in Missouri, Kansas, Washington Territory, and Texas. He resigned in 1857 with the rank of 1st Lieutenant and started farming near Glade Spring Depot.

Upon the passage of the ordinance of secession he raised a company of cavalry, the Washington Mounted Rifles, with which he joined Stuart in the Valley and took part in the First Manassas campaign. At this time, Gen. J. E. Johnston declared that his company was the strongest in the First Virginia cavalry regiment, "not surpassed in discipline and spirit by any in the army," and recommended that Stuart be given brigade command and that Jones, "skillful, brave and zealous in a very high degree," should succeed to the colonelcy, with Fitzhugh Lee as lieutenant-colonel. Consequently, he became colonel of the First, upon the organization of Stuart's brigade, and in the spring of 1862 was entrusted by Stuart with important duties in watching the enemy from the Blue Ridge to the Potomac. He was watchful and vigorous and made the enemy feel his presence.

Soon afterward, being displaced by a regimental election, he was assigned to the Seventh regiment, Robertson's brigade. Rejoining Stuart in August, he distinguished himself in the Second Manassas campaign. His regiment fought splendidly at Brandy Station and won commendation on several other occasions. He participated in the raid around McClellan's army following the battle of Sharpsburg, and on 8 November, having been promoted brigadier general, was assigned command of Robertson's "Laurel Brigade," composed of the men who followed Ashby in the Valley. On December 29, 1862, he was assigned to command the Valley district, including his brigade and all other troops operating in that region, being selected for this post by Stonewall Jackson. With the cooperation of General Imboden, in April and May 1863 he successfully raided the Baltimore & Ohio railroad west of Cumberland, destroying an immense amount of public and railroad property.

The legendary partisan ranger John S. Mosby said this of Grumble Jones: "He was a stern disciplinarian, and devoted to duty. Under a rugged manner and impracticable temper, he had a heart that beat with warm impulses. To his inferiors in rank, he was just and kind, but too much inclined to (go against) the wishes and (to) criticize the orders of his superiors." J. E. B. Stuart called him the "best outpost officer in the army," meaning that he recognized Jones's talent for operating in a detached fashion.

Then joining Stuart with his splendid brigade, he bore the first shock. In both the morning and evening of 9 June 1863, his outfit the brunt of the battle in the famous cavalry fight of Brandy Station. His brigade actually ended the fight with more horses and more and better small arms than it had at the beginning. It also captured two regimental colors, a battery of three artillery pieces, and about 250 Union prisoners.[17]

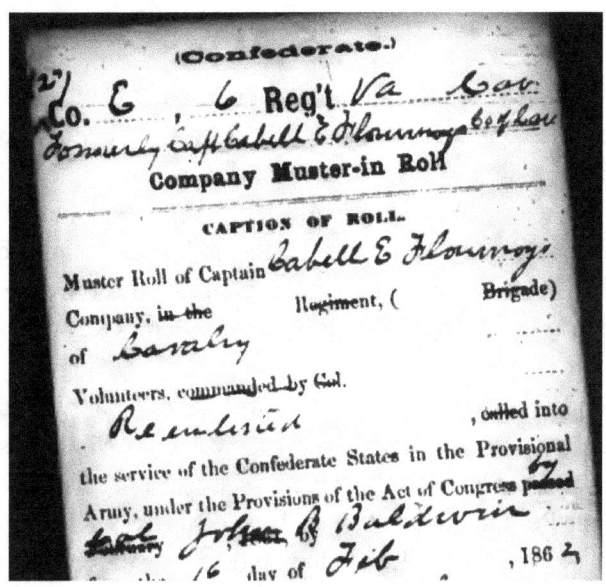

Major Cabell Edward Flournoy – 6th Virginia Cavalry

Cabell Flournoy was born on 30 June 1840 in Pittsylvania County, Virginia. Cabell was the son of U.S. Congressman Thomas Stanhope Flournoy, who also commanded Company G of the 6th Virginia upon the forming of that regiment. Little is known about Flournoy's early life in Virginia. The 1860 census lists him as a "law student," perhaps with thoughts of following his father's profession in politics. We can safely say that Cabell was excited to get into the war based on his offering of services to the governor of South Carolina prior to his home state of Virginia seceding. His men later referred to him as a "gallant young officer," but he was also described as enjoying a good drink and using colorful language – not too uncommon by today's standards.

The Pittsylvania Dragoons were organized on 7 January 1861 with young Cabell being made Captain. The company mustered into Confederate service five months later, on the 27 May 1861. Flournoy's company reported to camp of instruction at Ashland, Virginia, and received follow on orders to report to the western part of the state. The Dragoons would serve as an independent company under Roberts S. Garnett's command and later, under General Edward Johnson's. Here they fought in multiple engagements and learned the much-needed skills to be successful cavalry troopers, including organization and the art of supporting a command with cavalry.

In February 1862, Flournoy's time as an independent command ended when the company was assigned to the 6th Regiment of Virginia Cavalry. This assignment was influenced by his father, the former Congressman, and, at times, commander of the 6th Regiment, to which Cabell's company was assigned to the vacant "E" company slot. Captain Flournoy and his E company performed well as part of the 6th Regiment. Seeing action at Front Royal, Port Republic and Cross Keys, Flournoy fine tuned the company into an effective force. In July, having just celebrated his 22nd birthday, Cabell would be elected to the billet of regimental major with the reorganization of the brigade, to which the Sixth was assigned. Thomas Stanhope Flournoy of company G, Cabell's father, was named Colonel of the Regiment. It must have been an interesting dynamic to have father and son in key leadership billets of the same Regiment. Nevertheless, Colonel Flournoy proved a popular commander with his men and a capable tactician on the field. Official records indicate that the regiment performed well during the Second Manassas and Sharpsburg offensives.

All was going well for young Major Flournoy until an engagement at Paris, Virginia, on the 22 September 1862. Command of the regiment had passed to Lt. Colonel "Shac" Green as the elder Flournoy had departed the regiment on sick leave. This temporarily promoted Major Flournoy to the billet of Lieutenant Colonel and a whole new set of responsibilities. During the engagement, elements of the 1st Vermont Cavalry charged the Sixth Virginia. The Sixth stood motionless with pistols drawn and awaited the charge. One must wonder why Green did not order a countercharge or some other maneuver instead of standing in place to receive a mounted charge. Once the Vermonters were within pistol range, Green gave the command to fire. The results were not enough to stop the momentum of the mounted charge. The Sixth broke and began to fall back to the rear. Flournoy was observed in a position behind his men to keep them closed up. Others would interpret this as cowardice, or a shirking of duties. Either way, this would haunt Major Flournoy as it would follow him for months to come. The other result of this engagement was Flournoy's promotion to command the Sixth after Lt. Colonel Green was wounded and captured in the engagement at Paris. Flournoy would remain in command for just over three months until the parole and return of Lt. Colonel Green in January 1863.

The new year saw Major Flournoy preparing the regiment for campaign service in the Valley. Flournoy spent the initial months with his men on picket duty and patrolling, a boring task, but one that permitted the major time to refit the regiment with much needed resources. Flournoy accompanied his troops during raids into western Virginia in the months of April and May.

The Brigade commander, General Jones, was less than pleased with the performance of the regiment during its most recent expedition, however. He filed charges of disobedience against Lt. Colonel Green for poor performance during the fight at the Baltimore and Ohio Railroad bridge over the Cheat River. Flournoy was neither charged nor singled out, but surely was looked poorly upon by his brigade commander. Upon the brigade's return to the Valley in May, Jones ordered a board to convene and examine the current officers in "acting" billets of the 6th Regiment and review their promotions as officers of the regiment. This included reviewing proficiency in cavalry tactics and regulations. Flournoy, being the elected major and acting lieutenant colonel, was one of the officers reviewed by the board. He attended the proceedings and was permitted to cross-examine the officers who were testifying. As the regimental history of the 6th Virginia Cavalry describes Flournoy's examination:

> Eight officers, beginning with Green, testified about the major. Green thought him to be efficient, but discerned a prejudice against him, and thought that the murmurings of

the men showed a want of discipline when they were under him. Green admitted he had heard Flournoy's courage doubted, but cross-examination and later testimony made clear that this was because the major had left the center of the regiment during the Paris fight, on Lt. John W. Woolick's advice, to stop stragglers ... The board concluded that the major should be relieved from duty as soon as practicable and that he be assigned to other duties.[18]

The following day, Flournoy appealed to Gen. Jones in writing, calling the actions of the board "patently illegal." He further stated the majority of the regiment's officers found him "quite acceptable" as the regiment's major. Flournoy included a petition signed by 28 of the regiment's officers testifying to their approval of Flournoy as the Regimental Major. But Flournoy's appeal, and the decision of the board, had to be postponed when the Laurel Brigade was ordered to join Stuart's Division in Culpeper.

(Left) Lt. Colonel Thomas A. Marshall Jr. – 7th Virginia Cavalry

Thomas Marshall, Jr. was born on 17 January 1826. He was the grandson of Chief Justice of the U.S. Supreme Court John Marshall. He came from a family of "Virginians" of deep religious faith. He grew up at Oakhill, the Marshall estate in Fauquier County, Virginia. He attended Leeds Episcopal Church in Markham, where a marker near the entrance bears his name along with other soldiers who attended services there, including Turner Ashby. In 1845, Marshall enrolled at the University of Virginia and upon graduation went on to study law in Winchester. While there, he met Anna Maria Barton, the daughter of the lawyer Marshall was studying with. They married on 24 August 1848. She died twelve years later, at the age of 31. When Virginia passed its Ordinance of Secession in April of 1861, the 34-year-old Marshall volunteered his services to Virginia and was appointed a captain and served as an aide to Colonel Thomas Jackson – Stonewall Jackson – at Harpers Ferry. Marshall had opposed secession but felt a higher duty to Virginia and believed it was his place to serve.

Thomas Marshall's service record shows him as a man who was not afraid to lead from the front and be in the thick of the fight. Perhaps it was his strong Christian beliefs that encouraged him to be so brave in face of the enemy? "He was seen kneeling on the roadside for his morning prayer in the presence of the whole brigade. A few days later, going into a fight, he led the charge and stayed among the enemy until they were forced to retreat. From that time on when he knelt to pray, no one made a noise." Injuries among the horses he rode and to the man himself bespoke his direct exposure to danger. At the Battle of First Manassas, his horse was killed, the first of four, and at Orange Court House he was wounded by a saber blow to the head, the first of four wounds he would receive during the war.

After Manassas, Marshall resigned from his position on Jackson's staff to recruit a company for the spring 1862 campaign. Captain Marshall and his company were assigned to the command of Turner Ashby and performed well in early 1862. Upon the reorganization of the 7th Cavalry, and forming of the 12th Cavalry, Marshall was considered for the colonel billet of the newly formed 12th Regiment, but Marshall was instead promoted to the major's billet of the 7th Cavalry. The 7th would be assigned to Beverly Robertson's cavalry brigade. In August of the same year, Marshall suffered the severe head wound at Orange Court House. Having fractured his skull after being knocked "senseless," Marshall was captured and sent to Old Capitol Prison but was paroled in September and later exchanged before reporting back to the 7th Cavalry for duty. On 30

October, Marshall was appointed Lt. Colonel of the Regiment just before it was assigned to a new brigade led by William "Grumble" Jones.

When the 7th went into winter quarters, Lt. Colonel Marshall was assigned to court martial duty and remained there until January, when the regiment resumed more aggressive patrolling up and down the Valley. Marshall was present for the Jones-Imboden Raid into western Virginia in March and April and led an expedition into Greenland Gap in late April. The regiment's commanding officer, Colonel Dulaney, was wounded leading an assault against a fixed enemy position. This left Marshall as acting commander of the regiment for the remainder of the raid and for the movement east for the upcoming Gettysburg campaign.

(Left) Colonel Lunsford Lindsay Lomax – 11th Virginia Cavalry

Lunsford Lindsay Lomax was born on 4 November 1835 in Newport, Rhode Island. He was the son of Major Mann Page Lomax, a career Army officer. Lomax, like Thomas Marshall, descended from some of Virginias earliest families. His great-grandfather was an early plantation owner in Caroline County and had served in the Virginia House of Burgesses. Lomax's grandfather served in the Virginia House of Delegates. After a private education, Lomax received an appointment to West Point, where he graduated in 1856 and was assigned to the 2nd U.S. Cavalry in Kansas. Lomax resigned his commission on 25 April 1861 and was appointed a captain in the Virginia state forces. He initially served on the staff of Gen. Joseph H. Johnston, and then transferred to Brigadier General Benjamin McCulloch's staff. In April 1862, Lomax was promoted to lieutenant colonel and transferred to the staff of Major General Earl Van Dorn. He later served as Inspector General for the Army of East Tennessee.[19]

In February 1863, Lomax was promoted to colonel and a month later was given command of the newly formed 11th Virginia Cavalry. Lomax arrived in Virginia in time to participate in the Jones-Imboden raid into western Virginia. It must have been an imposing task to assume command of a cavalry regiment just stepping off on an expedition when he had not had a cavalry command for two years, and never a command of this size. To complicate matters, the lieutenant colonel of the 11th, Oliver Funsten, resigned after being passed over for command of the 11th following his command of the 17th Battalion of Virginia Cavalry prior to its expansion into a full regiment. This may have been the reason Funsten did not accompany the regiment on the raid but instead stayed behind with a detachment of men and horses who were "unfit" for the campaign. The after-action reports show that Funsten and his rear detachment had several encounters with the enemy and performed good service. Upon returning from the raid into western Virginia, the 11th was ordered to Strasburg, Virginia for picket duty and remained there until 1 June. The regiment returned to the former Brigade camp in Harrisonburg on 3 June and then followed in the tracks of the Laurel Brigade, which had already departed toward Culpeper to join up with Stuart's Cavalry Division.

(Left) Colonel Asher Waterman Harman – 12th Virginia Cavalry

Asher Harmon was born on 24 January 1830 in Waynesboro, Virginia. In his early adult life, he was the co-owner of a stage line along with his four brothers, all of whom served as commissioned officers in the Confederate service. In December 1852 he married Virginia Callaghan. He immediately volunteered for service after the state of Virginia seceded. On 28 April 1861, he was made Captain of

Company G of the 5th Virginia Infantry. He and his company served under Stonewall Jackson at Manassas in July and engaged in some of the heaviest fighting on Henry House Hill. During the months of September and October 1861, Harmon was listed as sick and at home. He returned to duty in November and December before being detached for quartermaster duty back in Staunton in January and February 1862.[20]

On 21 June 1862, Harmon was appointed colonel of the newly formed 12th Virginia Cavalry. The *Rockingham Register* newspaper wrote of Harmon's new appointment "he has the nerve, the will, the energy, the sagacity and the intelligence that make up the character of the successful military leader."[21] It is unclear why Harmon, an infantry officer, was selected to lead the new cavalry regiment. Did Jackson play a role?[22] Harmon's initial assignment was outpost duty in the Shenandoah Valley for the month of July. August brought orders to join Jackson's Army east of the Blue Ridge. Harmon would lead his men in action at Cedar Mountain that month and at Stevensburg on the 20 August. Later that month, the 12th took part in the Raid at Catlett's Station, and the Second Battle of Manassas.

The 12th had performed well and received compliments to fact from their brigade commander, Beverly Robertson. In early September 1862, the Army moved into Maryland and with that the 11th was assigned to move alongside, screening the Army. During this time, the regiment detached approximately 50 percent of its strength under Major Massie to remain in the Valley for a presence there. On 8 and 9 September, the remainder of the 11th experienced its first battlefield setbacks by being bested by the Federals near Poolesville. Thomas Munford was the acting brigade commander and stated that the 11th "behaved very badly." To add further sting, the 12th lost its regimental colors during the fighting on 9 September to the 8th Illinois Cavalry.[23] The 12th would redeem some of its honor on 14 September at Crampton's Gap, where a combined force of 500 dismounted men held off the entire Union 6th Corps for three hours. Colonel Munford praised their performance: "splendidly under the fire they were placed, [and doing] good service with their rifles."[24] For the remainder of the Maryland campaign, Colonel Harmon led the 11th on screening duties back into Virginia. Harmon's efforts were then focused on recruiting and resupplying his badly depleted regiment.

During this time, the 12th was assigned picket duty in the lower Shenandoah Valley, which aided Harmon's recruiting and resupply mission. The winter remained uneventful for full regimental encounters that would require Harmon's direct leadership. However, the spring of 1863 heated up with the famous Jones-Imboden raids. The 12th performed well during this time, mostly in supporting roles, until 25 April, when Harmon was given an assignment to lead a combined force. General Jones split his raiding force, with Harmon commanding one element and Jones the other. Harmon's orders were to press forward with his combined force to Oakland and burn the B&O Bridge. Harmon executed his orders, aggressively creating a path of destruction and destroying trestles and culverts alike while taking numerous prisoners and capturing horses. In 42 hours, Harmon's command traveled over 35 miles and accomplished every aspect of the mission.

Harmon's command reunited with Jones in the early morning hours of the 28 April. He received yet another leadership opportunity, to command the 11th Virginia and an independent battalion along with his own 12th Regiment to raid West Union. Jones's element would move west toward Cairo, while Harmon's command would push 26 miles northwest to destroy the railroad located there. Harmon found an enemy force in West Union numbering 400 to 500 men. Harmon employed a tactic of fixing the enemy in place with one element, while maneuvering around the flank with the second element. This proved to be of great success, with the destruction of railroad bridges east and west of town. To add to the success, Harmon's men captured a herd of cattle as they retrograded south. The command linked back with Jones on the 9 May and the combined force continued operations by burning the oil stores on the Kanawha River without incurring any casualties. On 14 May, Harmon would get yet a third opportunity for independent command. This mission was one of logistics with a much smaller command, but still more opportunities to expand Harmon's overall leadership abilities. Harmon would proceed to Staunton to forward supplies to Warm Springs. Upon completion of his last mission in support of the raid, Harmon's command would link back up with the

Laurel Brigade in camp outside of Harrisonburg to rest and refit. The 11th Virginia cavalry stepped off with the brigade on 1 June for the movement east toward Culpeper.

(Left) Lt. Colonel Elijah Viers White – 35th Battalion of Virginia Cavalry

Elijah "Lige" White was born on the 29th August 1832, just west of Poolesville, Maryland. He was the son of Stephen Newton White and Mary Viers. He was educated at Lima Seminary in New York followed by attending Granville College (later Denison University) in Ohio, from which he graduated in 1854. White sought excitement and adventure by participating in the Kanas-Missouri border conflict as part of a Missouri volunteer company. In 1856, after a year in Missouri, White returned to his native area and purchased a farm north of Leesburg, Virginia. In 1857, he married Sarah Elizabeth Gott and the couple settled into a life of farming.

White stayed active with the local militia and enlisted in Captain Shreve's company of Loudon Cavalry as a private. He rose to the rank of corporal before transferring to Captain Mason's company that would soon become G company of the 7th Virginia Cavalry Regiment. In October 1861, White was granted leave to return home. While there, Federal troops crossed the river near Ball's Bluff bringing on an engagement. White, being nearby and knowing the area very well, volunteered his service to Colonel Nathan Evans, who was the commander at Leesburg. Evans assigned White to Colonel Eppa Hutton's headquarters, where he served as a scout, courier, and guide. White excelled at his tasks and won commendations from three separate commanders.[25]

Impressed by White's actions, Evans strongly encouraged White to apply for a commission in regular Army. White did so but was denied a regular commission. Instead, he was given a commission as captain in the

Provisional Army and authorized to raise a company of irregulars for border service in his native Loudon County. White quickly began recruiting and, with the first fifteen men, began running a series of couriers between Leesburg and Winchester. By the end of March, White had recruited enough in numbers to become a company and was regularly organized with the assistance of Colonel Thomas Munford, a Virginia Military Institute graduate. Munford would stay on until the end of April, mentoring White in organization, sustainment, discipline, and organization.

White's command was attached to General Richard Ewell's headquarters to serve as couriers and scouts. In April, White received his first wound, shot in face by another Confederate who did not recognize him and his men as friendlies. White returned to his command in late June and linked up with the Army just after the battle of Gaines Mill. Word of White's exploits reached back to the Loudon border area, creating much excitement. This sparked volunteers who sought out and joined White in numbers great enough for a second company to be formed in late August. His command now numbered close to 100 men. White's men would move with the Army north, into Maryland, for the September campaign. This provided another opportunity to recruit able bodies men to the ranks of White's irregulars. At Frederick, White issued a proclamation:

> Marylanders to the Rescue!
>
> I am a Marylander ... I have been in the service eighteen months, opposing the tyranny which would have made of the South a subjugated and ruined country. I came to Maryland with the Southern Army to do what I can to carry where she belongs, to the Southern Confederacy. I want Marylanders to join me. I am authorized to raise a regiment of Maryland Cavalry. I have no recruiting office. I can be found at Gen. Lawton's headquarters where I will be happy to receive recruits. Come at once or make up your minds to be slaves to Northern despotism forever.
>
> E. V. White
>
> Captain Commanding Gen. Lawton's Bodyguard
>
> September 8, 1862[26]

White and his "Rebels" performed good service during the Maryland campaign operating in small detachments and performing numerous functions of irregular cavalry. White was wounded again on 17 September during fighting in the town of Leesburg, Virginia. In his absence, recruits were still coming in, making total numbers that approached battalion-size strength. Unfortunately, discipline, morale and battlefield success suffered as White was recuperating from his recent wound. This shows how great an effect White's leadership had on this group of partisans. Always keeping the men in line an accepting nothing less than victory was White's way of leading.

In mid-October, White, still in his sick bed, was ordered to prepare for organization as a battalion. On 28 October 1862, White's Rebels were mustered in as the 35th Battalion of Virginia Cavalry, a full five companies. With the expansion came his promotion to major. In November, White's Battalion was assigned to the headquarters of Brigadier General William Jones, future commander of the Laurel Brigade. White's Battalion enjoyed great success in raiding and scouting for the brigadier. Unfortunately for White's "irregulars," they would suffer the growing pains of becoming part of the regular brigade in January. White received assistance in the drilling, organization, administration, and discipline of his battalion through the efforts of Lieutenant Richard T. Watts of the 2nd Virginia Cavalry, Munford's regiment. White was promoted to lieutenant colonel at the end of January and would continue to lead his men through the reorganization process for the next two months. By April, the troopers of the 35th were standing daily inspections in preparation for the upcoming raids into western Virginia.

White, who enlisted as a private with no formal military training, had made great strides over the past couple of years. Today, one might describe White as a "natural leader." Men were drawn to his leadership, and he provided them with a confident presence on the battlefield. The battalion marched over 700 miles during the next 31 days of successful raiding in enemy occupied territory. Now a lieutenant colonel, White led his battalion into rest and refit as he prepared them for movement east into Culpeper with the rest of Laurel Brigade.

(Left) Captain Robert Preston Chew – Chew's Battery

Authors Note: I have elected to include the bio of Captain Chew in this chapter of the handbook. His battery of horse artillery accompanied the Laurel Brigade throughout the Valley and for the march into Culpeper before being assigned to battalion artillery of Stuart's Cavalry Division.

Robert Chew was born on 9 April 1843 in Loudon County, Virginia, and grew up in Charlestown (now in West Virginia). He attended Charlestown Academy and the Virginia Military Institute. With the outbreak of hostilities, Chew served as a drill master in Richmond in the spring of 1861. He next served as an "acting' lieutenant and adjutant for Harwicke's Battery of Virginia Light Artillery.

The 19 year-old Chew presented himself before his former VMI artillery instructor, Stonewall Jackson, to offer his service as a volunteer. At the suggestion of Turner Ashby, Chew was commissioned captain of an artillery battery. His battery was formed by special order of the Confederate government on 11 November 1861. The battery consisted of two artillery pieces of different sizes and 33 men. The battery would receive a third gun, a 12-pound howitzer, on 31 December. Private George Neese wrote of his initial meeting with Captain Chew shortly after joining the battery on 13 December: "I had an introduction to Captain Chew ... from the little conversation that I had with him, and from the soldier-like appearance of his environments and his gentlemanly deportment, together with the courteous welcome he gave me as a stranger to his command. I am almost convinced already that what I have done today will in the end prove to have been a prudent act, as I will be under the immediate command of one who has studied the art of war."

Snow fell on the Harpers Ferry District in January 1862, creating challenges for the new battery not only with the training of the men and horses but with moving cannons about in the slick snow and mud. At the end of January, the battery moved to Martinsburg, and then weeks later, to Winchester as warmer weather moved in. In early spring, the battery was attached to Ashby's cavalry for operations in the Valley. Here the young Captain Chew learned to master his craft of horse artillery while supporting the ever-aggressive Ashby. In 1862, Chew and his battery saw combat at Kernstown, Harrisonburg, Port Republic, the Second Manassas Campaign, and the Maryland Campaign. The battery finished out the year with General Jones, who assumed command of the Laurel Brigade, with operations in Front Royal, Charlestown, Winchester, Strasburg, and finally Moorefield before going into winter quarters in January. Captain Chew and his Battery did not participate in the Jones-Imboden raids of April and May due to heavy rains and uncrossable rivers. He was kept busy in the Harrisonburg area until the return of the Laurel Brigade in May. When the brigade stepped off for Culpeper, Chew and his well-seasoned battery joined them.

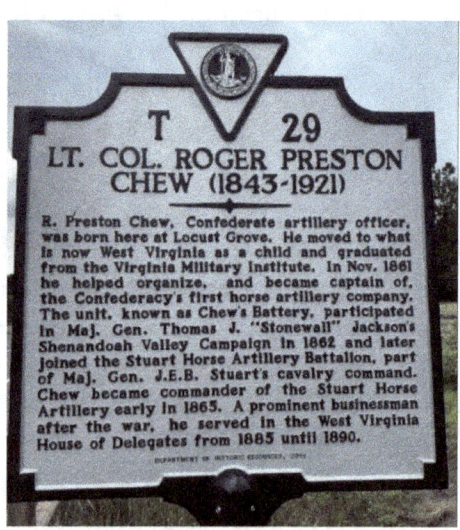

State Historic Marker,
intersection Harry Bird Highway and Williams Gap Road

Chapter 3

The March to Culpeper

To understand why the Laurel Brigade was ordered to join J. E. B. Stuart's cavalry and the Army of Northern Virginia, we must briefly look at the strategic level of war situation in May 1863. In December 1862, and then again in early May 1863, the Army of Northern Virginia won two great victories over the Federal forces of the Army of the Potomac. General Lee had again been able to out general his opponent. But with those victories came the loss of manpower and material resources that could not be easily replaced. The Federal forces had a much better infrastructure in place to resupply the Army of the Potomac and a far larger population to draw from. In a strategic analysis, what did Confederate forces in Northern Virginia really gain from their two most recent victories? The Army of Northern Virginia was still in the same area, and it was consuming resources at the cyclic rate. General Lee had to plan to go on the offensive or continue to serve as roadblock to Richmond from Federal forces.

General Lee realized that keeping the Army in its current position would lead to defeat as it would be out resourced and eventually outmaneuvered by remaining static.[27] General Lee proposed a plan to seize the initiative and presented a plan to the Confederate leadership in Richmond.[28]

Following a series of meetings held after the Battle of Chancellorsville, the Confederate leadership decided that the time was right for another invasion of the North. A northward thrust would serve a variety of purposes: First, it could potentially relieve Federal pressure on the beleaguered Southern garrison at Vicksburg. Second, it would provide the people of Virginia with an opportunity to recover from "the ravages of war and a chance to harvest their crops free from interruption by military operation." Third, it would draw the Federals, now under Joseph Hooker, away from its base at Falmouth, giving Lee an opportunity to defeat it in the open field. Finally, as historian Edwin B. Coddington put it, Lee "wanted to spend the summer in lower Pennsylvania maneuvering his forces to pose threats to the vital centers of Washington, Baltimore, and Philadelphia, while stripping the country of needed supplies."[29]

Following his decision to invade the North, Lee began shifting troops west for a move through the Shenandoah Valley, an operation set for 3 June. Almost immediately, rumors of this activity began trickling into Union headquarters. On 27 May, Colonel George H. Sharpe of the Provost Marshal General's office and chief of intelligence for the Army of the Potomac, reported, "There are three brigades of cavalry 3 miles from Culpeper County Court House, toward Kelly's Ford ... These are Fitz. Lee's, William H. Fitzhugh Lee's, and Wade Hampton's brigades ... The Confederate army is under marching orders, and an order from General Lee was very lately read to the troops, announcing a campaign of long marches and hard fighting."

On 23 May, Lee wrote General William Jones to congratulate him on his recent raid into western Virginia. He also ordered him to report to Stuart's Cavalry Division at Culpeper. Jones was clearly upset with the orders to serve alongside Stuart again and offered his resignation to Gen. Lee. Lee clearly recognized the value of Jones at the head of Laurel Brigade and retained the resignation but did not accept it. Lee acknowledged Jones's displeasure with his new assignment but preferred to keep him at the head of his brigade.

On 1 June, the Laurel Brigade began the 70-mile trek to Culpeper arriving on 3 and 4 June. The following chapter will begin the staff ride in Dayton, Virginia, where the Laurel Brigade was camped prior to moving out toward Culpeper. This will provide the reader with the opportunity to cover the same ground, outside of the built-up areas around Harrisonburg, as did the Laurel Brigade in the first days of June 1863, and sites of the subsequent fighting that occurred at Brandy Station. Some readers may wish to skip the first section of stops, 1A to 1E, and move directly to Stop 2, and start at Brandy Station.

Chapter 4

The Staff Ride

Stop 1A – Laurel Brigade Camp Dayton – Dove Park

Orientation: The staff ride begins at Dove Park 360 College Street in Dayton, Virginia. The park has ample parking and restroom facilities, with a large map of Dayton to aid in orientation. North is in the direction of the high ground past the restrooms. There is a large farm on top of the hill to the north. Immediately east, across the open pasture, is the wartime Daniel Harrison farm. The road across the pasture that runs past the Harrison farm is the Warm Springs Turnpike, which dates to 1833. The area where you are standing is the 1863 edge of town. The camp of the Laurel Brigade was a half mile distant to the north, just past Cooks Creek. One can imagine the size of a camp for a 2,000-man plus brigade of cavalry. The men, horses, mules, and logistics must have required a great deal of ground and resources to sustain the brigade during its time here.

Note: It is suggested you bring a compass, a map of the area, binoculars, and GPS to aid in the execution of the staff ride.

(Left) Entrance sign for park (Author's "photo" vice Authors "collection")

From 20 May until the morning of 1 June, the Laurel Brigade was camped in this area. It is an excellent selection for a cavalry camp, with nearby Cooks Creek providing fresh water. The high ground, with excellent drainage, is still ideal for horse picket lines and grazing pastures. The nearby Warm Springs Turnpike provides means for supply wagons to transit on an improved road. Note: The 11th Virginia Cavalry was on detached duty to Strasburg, Virginia.

Proceed north on foot to just past the wall map to the fence line. You will be able to get a clear view of the camp location on the high ground.

**Looking north towards camp.
Harrison farm is seen to the right.
(Author's "photo" vice Authors "collection")**

George M. Neese of Chew's Battery kept an excellent diary record of the movement east: "June 1 – This morning we left our camp in Dayton and are now bound for eastern, Virginia, where war seems to be in full bloom, and no doubt, we will soon be in the midst of the throes and struggles of sanguinary war and hear the dreadful crash of battle." Neese also described the route the brigade took through Harrisonburg and on to Standardsville Pike: "We passed through Harrisonburg and took the Standardsville Pike, marching 21 miles today."

(Left) George M. Neese of Chew's Battery

Proceed by car to the next stop. Pull out of the parking lot making a right and head North for about 150 feet, then turn right onto College Street. Off to your left/north, you will have a nice view of the Laurel Brigade camp area on high ground. Cross Route 11 and proceed to Stone Spring Road to Spotswood Trail/modern day Highway 33. Stay on Highway 33 for approximately 15 miles until you reach modern day Elkton, formerly Conrads Store. See Stop 1B for specific directions to the camp site. The drive to stop 1B will take you about 30 to 35 minutes.

Stop 1B – Laurel Brigade Camp near Elkton –

Orientation: This camp site has been developed and is now lost. However, you will get a sense of the distance traveled on the first day's march. The campsite is located on the east bank of the Shenandoah River. Take the exit off Spotswood Trail for Southeast Side Highway. Take a left off the exit onto Southeast Side Highway, followed by a right onto West Summit Ave. You will now be in a built-up neighborhood, none of buildings in which were here in 1863. After two blocks, the road will become a dead end. Feel free to pull over but be respectful of the homeowners and private property. North is the direction of Spotswood Trail from which you drove in. The Shenandoah River is to the west. You are now just east of the river and at the approximate location of the Laurel Brigade Camp.

The Brigade rode into camp after a 21-mile march, camping approximately 17 miles east of Harrisonburg. Here they set in for the night, camping in an area they had camped the previous April, on ground familiar to them. The proximity to the river provided water for both troopers and horses.

George Neese describes the next morning's movement east: "June 2 – We renewed our march this morning and crossed the Blue Ridge at Swifts Run Gap. We marched to Standardsville and there turned off on Madison Courthouse Road. Moved out five miles from Standardsville and camped. Our camp is in the edge of Madison County."

Return to your vehicle and make your way back to Highway 33 East/Spotswood Trail. You will enter the Shenandoah National Forest and pass over the Blue Ridge. Use caution as the road will become steep and have tight curves in spots. Follow the Highway in a southeasterly direction for 15 miles until you reach Standardsville by taking 33 Business. Here you will turn and head north on Madison Road. After a few miles, the road will turn into Wolfton-Hood Road. You will cross the South River, and about five miles on you will reach the Roaring Twenties Antique Car Museum. It is slightly past the Green Hills Club and the county line. Pull into the museum's parking lot on your left and park.

Parking lot sign for museum (Author's "photo" vice Authors "collection")

Stop 1C – Laurel Brigade Camp Green/Madison County Line –

Orientation: Get out of your vehicle and face back toward the direction from which you drove in. North is in the opposite direction of which you are facing. The location of Laurel Brigade camp is about a half mile in the distance to the south. It stretches down to the area that is currently the Green Hills Club. The modern camp area is mostly wooded with nothing of note to mark the camp location.

Chapter 4

**View looking back toward the direction of camp
(Author's "photo" vice Authors "collection")**

George Neese spoke of the rain and poor road conditions they faced the following morning: "June 3 – Rained last night, which made the red and yellow clay in these Tuckeyhoe roads almost as sticky as shoemaker's wax."

Note: The 11th Virginia Cavalry left Harrisonburg on 3 June enroute to rejoin the rest of the brigade.[30]

Once you are done viewing the area, return to your vehicle and resume driving north by east on the Wolfton-Hood Road. When you reach the intersection of U.S. 29, divided highway, turn left and resume a northern direction. Just past the high school, on your right, the road will split to your left providing you the opportunity to drive through Madison and follow the Laurel Brigade's original route of march.

George Neese provided an excellent description of the route of the march:

> We renewed our march this morning. Early in the day we passed Wolftown, a little hamlet of some six houses ...
> We passed through Madison Courthouse today. The town is situated on a wave-like swell, elevated above the surrounding country. The houses are comparatively small, and most, or all of them, are built of wood. The town in general is on the scattered order.

Upon exiting the town of Madison, merge back onto 29 and continue heading north by east. Just past Brightwood is the area of Leon. This area was James City in 1863. Look for a "Civil War Trails" marker on your right in Leon. Turn onto Leon Road, Virginia, Route 631. Pull into the parking area on your left.

Sign at parking area. (Author's "photo" vice Authors "collection")

Stop 1D – Laurel Brigade Camp Bethel Church – near Madison, Virginia

Orientation: Get out of your vehicle and face back toward Route 29. You are looking in the general direction of North. You are less than ten miles from Culpeper to the east. The exact location of the Laurel Brigade camp is not known, but they were camped in this general vicinity. Behind you is a mid-19th century home that was a part of James City. One may wonder if some of the officers of the Laurel Brigade might have stayed in the home or camped with their men on these very grounds?

George Neese provided an accurate description of James City: "This afternoon we passed through a small nest of a village sporting the name of James City. It is situated in a rolled-up country in the western part of Culpeper County. We crossed Robinson River today in Madison County. We are camped this evening at Bethel Church, nine miles from Culpeper Court House."

**19th century home of James City
(Author's "photo" vice Authors "collection")**

Return to your vehicle and proceed toward Culpeper Court House on Route 29. Stay on Route 29/James Madison Highway until you reach the edge of town. Take the turn onto Madison Road and follow it to Main Street. Continue on Main Street through town and then turn right onto east Piedmont Street. Drive three blocks and then turn left onto Old Brandy Road. Follow the road as it curves to the right. Just past the curve is Wine Street. Turn onto Wine Street and parallel park on the street. To your left is Wine Street Memorial Park.

Park sign (Author's "photo" vice Authors "collection")

Stop 1E – Laurel Brigade Camp east of Culpeper – Wine Street Memorial Park

Orientation: Exit your vehicle, cross the street, and proceed to Memorial Park. As you are facing the monument, you are looking east, and North is to your left. This is the location of the Laurel Brigade's camp on the evening of 4 June 1863. In areas that are now populated with homes, 1,600 troopers were encamped along with horses, mules, wagons, artillery pieces with limber, caissons, and battery wagons.

Just beyond the monument is the area where the brigade camped. (Author's "photo" vice Authors "collection")

George Neese: "June 4 – We renewed our march this morning and moved to Culpeper Court House…Culpeper Court House is a pretty town pleasantly situated on the gently rising slope of a hill in a rolling and diversified section of the country. West of the town toward the Blue Ridge the country is broken by wooded ridges, but looking east and south toward the lower Rapidan the country is beautiful and open, the land being level and of good quality. The town is situated on the Orange and Alexandria Railroad about nine miles from the Rappahannock River. It contains about one thousand inhabitants. Main Street is wide and straight and in general appearance it resembles an embryo city street. We are camped this evening half mile east of Culpeper Court House."

The men of the Laurel Brigade, having just completed a 70-mile march, must have had mixed thoughts knowing that there would be no time for rest, but rather they had to prepare for the next day's "Grand Review," to be conducted by their division commander.

Below is an extract of a letter written by Lieutenant Thomas Marshall of E company, 12th Virginia Cavalry, to his wife, Bettie. He writes about the upcoming "Grand Review" to be held by General Stuart the following day on 5 June:

> June 4th, 1863
>
> My dear Bettie – I have just gotten your letter and sit down to write a short answer – Our cavalry had a skirmish yesterday with the Yankees as they attempted to cross the Rappahannock at Waterloo, I believe, and drove them back. We are having a grand review tomorrow at Brandy Station of all of Stewart's Cavalry. I reckon it will be an imposing sight. We are to have a sham fight and charge artillery loaded with blank cartridges. Divisions of infantry are making their appearance in these parts. We know nothing but the general impression is that there will be a forward move.

Return to your vehicle and turn back onto Old Brandy Road heading east. Drive 3.5 miles and pull off to the right onto gravel at the old RR Crossing location. It is ¼ of a mile before the Goodyear shop and a few hundred yards just past the Virginia State Police office.

Parking location next to O & A Railroad
(Author's "photo" vice Authors "collection")

Stop 2 – The Grand Review

Orientation: Exit your vehicle and face back towards Brandy Road. As you are facing Brandy Road, north is slightly to your right. The Brandy Station crossroads are just over a mile to your right/east. The campsite of the Laurel Brigade from which you just departed is 3.5 miles to your left/west. To your rear are the still active tracks of the Orange and Alexandria Railroad. Off in the distance, across Brandy Road and James Madison Highway/29, on the high ground to the north sits Auburn, the 2,200-acre farm owned by John Minor Botts in 1863. You are standing in the approximate location of the reviewing stand put in place for guests to observe the Grand Review of 5 June.

View of the "Grand Review" location. Auburn, the home of pro-Union John Minor Botts can be seen in the distance.
(Author's "photo" vice Authors "collection")

George Neese provided a description of the guest viewing area: "Hundreds of ladies from Culpeper Court House and surrounding country stood in bunches on hills and knolls around the field, looking at the grand military display. A special train from Richmond stood on the track just in rear of the review stand, crowded with people, and judging from fluttering ribbons at the car windows most of the occupants were ladies. General Hood's Division was drawn up on the north side of the field, viewing the cavalry display."

In accordance with General Lee's plan to invade Pennsylvania, his corps commanders James Longstreet and Richard S. Ewell had already begun their northward movement while A. P. Hill's III Corps remained behind to hold the Army of the Potomac, under Joseph Hooker, in place. Stuart's cavalry division was to cross the Rappahannock River on 9 June and screen east of Longstreet's and Ewell's advance. Stuart would move his division to Brandy Station to prepare for the upcoming campaign and take advantage of the grass available in the area to graze the division's horses.

While in Culpeper, Stuart held three grand reviews: on 22 May, 5 June, and 8 June, all conducted at Auburn Plantation. The 22 May review consisted of the brigades commanded by W. H. F. Rooney Lee, Fitzhugh Lee, and Wade Hampton. Beverly Robertson's North Carolina Brigade arrived at Brandy Station on 25 May and did not participate in the first review. The Laurel Brigade arrived on 3 and 4 June with the 11th Virginia Cavalry arriving on the 7th.

(Left) Wartime image of Auburn. Timothy H. O'Sullivan, Library of Congress

It must have been an impressive sight when all five brigades marshaled together. The line of Stuart's division, drawn up in two ranks, extended approximately two miles. But in the modern opinion of Colonel Joseph W. McKinney, "J. E. B. Stuart was roundly criticized for his grand reviews. This provides an opening to discuss training methods of the time (drill) and how commanders evaluated the training status and readiness of units (reviews)."[31]

Major General J. E. B. Stuart, Commanding Cavalry Division, Army of Northern Virginia, J. Gurney & Son, Library of Congress

General Lee was pleased, however, writing to his mother:

I reviewed the cavalry in this section yesterday. It was a splendid sight. The men and horses looked well. They have recuperated since last fall. Stuart was in all his glory.

Your sons and nephews were well and flourishing. The country here looks very green and pretty, notwithstanding the ravages of war. What a beautiful world God, in his loving kindness to His creatures, has given us! What a shame that men endowed with reason and knowledge of right should mar His gifts.

In response to Stuart's cavalry, displaced from Fredericksburg to the Culpeper area, Hooker swung into action. He ordered his cavalry commander, Brigadier General Alfred Pleasonton, to advance his 11,000-man corps against Stuart's 10,000 cavalry. The plan was to converge at Culpeper, crossing the Rappahannock at Beverly and Kelly's Fords. Pleasonton's orders were straightforward: he was to "disperse and destroy" the Confederate cavalry in the Culpeper area.

Major General Joseph Hooker
Library of Congress

Brigadier General Alfred Pleasonton
Library of Congress

The next stop will be the picket post of Company A of the 6th Virginia Cavalry at Beverly Ford, at the convergence of the Hazel and Rappahannock Rivers. Return to your vehicle and resume driving east on Brandy Road. In just over a mile, you will turn left onto Alanthus Road and immediately come to a four-way stop light intersection at James Madison Highway. Cross over the intersection and just past the park-and-ride, and then make a right turn onto Fleetwood Heights Road. Drive for 1.8 miles and then turn left onto Cobb's Legion Road followed by another left onto Beverly Ford Road. You will pass the Culpeper airport on your right and shortly thereafter the paved road will turn to gravel. Reduce speed and proceed for another half mile down the gravel road. Park at the "End State Maintenance" sign. The area around you is private land so be respectful of the landowners and do not cross the split-rail fence.

Just beyond these signs is the location of Captain Gibson's picket line. (Author's "photo" vice Authors "collection")

Stop 3 – Captain Gibson's Picket line – Near Beverly Ford

Orientation: You are now near the location of Captain Bruce Gibson's 60-man picket line. The direction from which you arrived, and are now facing, is North. The Beverly Ford Crossing on the Rappahannock and Hazel Rivers is to your direct front, another ¼ mile distant across the field. The river is about 3½ feet deep with steep banks. Company A has constructed a strong barricade of rails along the edge of the wood just off the riverbank. To your rear, where the pavement changed to gravel, was the location of Beckham's Battalion of Horse artillery. Further beyond that, near the southern edge of the airport, is where the troopers of the

Laurel Brigade camped.[32] The 7th Virginia of the Laurel Brigade was serving as part of the "Grand Guard," better known today as a quick reaction force, QRF.

Stuart positioned his cavalry division to screen the pending movements of the army for offensive operations in Pennsylvania. The division headquarters stood at Fleetwood Heights, about one mile and half to the rear of the Laurel Brigade's camp. To the immediate north of the Laurel Brigade camp was the brigade of Brigadier General W. H. F. Rooney Lee and beyond that, a few miles further to the North, was Brigadier General Fitzhugh Lee's Virginia brigade (temporarily under the command of Colonel Thomas Munford due to Lee's debilitating rheumatoid arthritis), with one regiment detached screening the rear of the division near Stevensburg. To the South of the Laurel Brigade camp was Wade Hampton's brigade, also with one regiment detached near Stevensburg. Hampton's camp was in the vicinity of the southern end of modern-day Culpeper Airport. Brigadier General Beverly Robertson's Brigade is to the Southeast, beyond Newby's Shop toward Kellysville guarding the crossing at Kelly's Ford. Near Culpeper Court House was General John Bell Hood's infantry division of about 7,000 men. Hood's troops formed some of the lead elements of the Army of Northern Virginia's main body that is moving North.

Luther W. Hopkins of Company A describes the opening engagement:

> I was on picket duty at one of the fords, and was relieved at 3 o'clock in the morning, another soldier taking my place. I went up through the field into the woods where our reserves (some 20 men) were in camp. It was from this squadron that pickets were sent out and posted along the river. I hitched my horse and wrapped in a blanket, lay down to sleep. But I was so rudely awakened by the watchman, who shouted that the enemy was crossing the river. We all jumped up and mounted our horses. Our captain was with us. The day was just breaking. The pickets were hurrying up from the river in every direction, firing their pistols to give the alarm.

Luther W. Hopkins, Company A, 6th Virginia Cavalry

Two brothers, Robert and Fleet James were on duty at Beverly Ford while the remaining pickets rested about a hundred yards to the rear. The resting troopers on picket duty kept their horses saddled and carbines ready even while sleeping. At 0430, the sun was not yet rising and the misty fog on the river further limited visibility. All that could be heard was the water rushing over the "crib" dam just upstream. Out of the morning mist advanced troopers of the 6th New York Cavalry. They came on at a walk in what was belly deep water of the horses. Yet the advance was masked by the elements and caught the Fleet brothers by surprise.

Recognizing their position was untenable, the brothers rode back toward the main picket line, firing their pistols to alert their fellow Company A troopers. As the Fleet boys fell back, the 6th New York secured the crossing and conducted a forward passage of lines with the 8th New York followed by the 8th Illinois Cavalry. Pursuit was delayed as the river crossing slowed the Federal build up and limited maneuver space.

Captain Gibson, "a brave and prudent officer," calmly waited as the New Yorkers advanced on the Beverly Ford Road. He ordered his men onto their horses and sent a courier back the main camp area to alert them of the danger. He steadied his men and instructed them "shoot to kill." When the enemy presented himself, Gibson gave the command to fire. The volley blasted the advancing New Yorkers, inflicting multiple casualties, including Lieutenant Henry Clay Cutler of Company B, 8th New York, who was shot in the neck. Gibson's troopers would only briefly delay the advancing troopers in Blue. Quickly, Capt. Gibson ordered his men to fall back down the road toward friendly lines, leaving two men dead on the field.

CAPTAIN BRUCE GIBSON
6th Virginia Cavalry

Postwar image of Captain Bruce Gibson, Company A, 6th Virginia Cavalry, Mount Hebron Cemetery

As fighting broke out at Beverly Ford, Major Flournoy was getting his troopers into the saddle and galloping toward the sound of the guns. Major Beckham's horse artillery was also alerted and busily catching horses and limbering up guns.

The Federal advance was led by Colonel Benjamin F. "Grimes" Davis. He commanded the 1st Brigade of Brigadier General John Buford's Cavalry Division. Davis organized his two regiments on the road by ordering up the 8th Illinois onto the New Yorkers left. With both regiments riding abreast, in a column of fours, they advanced in pursuit of Gibson's fleeing company.

Colonel Benjamin F. Davis, Library of Congress

The road trace of Beverly Ford Road is mostly the same today as it was in 1863. As you retrace your route to the next stop, you are following the route of Colonel Grimes's advance.

The map below shows the position of Gibson's picket line, Beckham's Horse artillery camp, and the direction of the advancing Federal Cavalry.

Chapter 4

Map from Library of Congress, William W. Blackford, Graphics by author

Return to your vehicle and drive south down the gravel road until you reach the American Battlefield Trust parking circle on your right. Pull into the traffic circle and park in the designated area. Exit your vehicle and move to a position of high ground for better observation in the direction of Beverly's Ford.

Entrance to American Battlefield Trust parking area.
(Author's "photo" vice Authors "collection")

Stop 4 – Beckham's Artillery Battalion camp – American Battlefield Trust parking lot

Orientation: You are at the location of Beckham's battalion of horse artillery camp on the evening of 8 June and morning of 9 June 1863. Here Beckham was directed to place his four batteries of artillery currently, McGregor's, Mormon's, Hart's, and Chew's. The mowed path by the interpretive markers is to the north. To your immediate south is Culpeper Airport. Beverly Ford is about a mile distant to the northeast. The camp of the Laurel Brigade is at Saint James Church to the west. It is suggested to move up the mowed grass path to high ground for better observation.

Captain Gibson's delaying action at Beverly Ford permitted Major Flournoy of the 6th Virginia to muster a force of 150 men. The Virginia troopers hastily mounted their horses, some without saddles, some only partially dressed: "Alfred Harrison Dwyer of Co. B made the charge wearing only his long johns." Flournoy quickly organized his men and led the charge to toward the ford: "Upon hearing this firing, Lieutenants George Shumate and Owen Allen of the 'Clarke Cavalry,' hastily formed the men who had horses in camp and ordered them to charge down the road." Lt. Colonel Thomas Marshall and his 7th Virginia Cavalry arrived just as Flournoy was departing and joined the 6th Virginia's counterattack, staying just west of the road. The Virginians, New Yorkers and troopers from Illinois all collided in the early morning hours just as the sun was beginning to rise.

John Newton Opie, of Company D of the 6th Virginia Cavalry was a participant in the charge:

> I mounted my wild charger for the last time, and fell in the first set of fours, when the order to charge was given, and we started down the road at a gallop. My horse did what I too well knew she would do – that is, she shot out from the column like a thunderbolt and rushed down the road with the rapidity of lightning. I looked around behind me, and no one was in sight … I turned a bend in the road, and there, across my path, was a double line of cavalry.

John N. Opie in his VMI Cadet uniform, late a Rebel cavalryman

Luther W. Hopkins described the scene as he fell back with Company A:

> As we came out of the woods into the fields, we met the Sixth Virginia Regiment, under Col. Flournoy, coming down the road at full gallop. Just on his left, and on a line with the Sixth, was the Seventh Virginia Regiment coming across the fields. These two regiments entered the woods, one on the right and one on the left, and stretching out on either side, poured a volley into the advancing enemy that caused them to halt for a while.

The 6th Virginia sustained approximately 30 casualties during the early morning fight on Beverly Ford Road. Flournoy had to withdraw as he was outnumbered and in danger of being outflanked. Yet a blow had been dealt to Davis's Federal troopers and their advance stalled. By all accounts, Flournoy was a man of interesting character.[33] Operating under unknown circumstances on the morning of 9 June, (the review board's decision had relieved him as commander of the 6th), he made an quick decision and saved J. E. B. Stuart's artillery battalion from capture by charging down the road and allowing Beckham's artillery to pull back, away from immediate threat.

As Flournoy fell back, Lieutenant Owen Allen, Company D, observed the Federal force from the edge of the woods just where the road bends. He spotted Grimes Davis, several yards out in front of his troopers. Davis was focused on rallying his regiments and regaining the advance and was unaware of any threats. Lieutenant Allen, recognizing Davis as a senior officer, galloped up toward him from his blind side with a pistol drawn. Davis's last words were reported "Stand firm, Eighth New York!" Davis must have heard Allen's advance as he turned and instinctively swung his saber, which Allen avoided while simultaneously firing his pistol. Davis was struck in the head by Allen's shot, killing him almost immediately. The senior Federal officer south of the river was now dead. Sergeant John Stone, also of Company D, engaged in the brief mele as a Federal trooper rode up and delivered a mortal saber blow that cut Stone "midway between eyes and chin."

The New York and Illinois cavalrymen were temporarily leaderless after Davis's death. With Confederate artillery deployed in the road, the Union attack stalled and the Federals fell back to regroup. Major William S. McClure, commanding the 3rd Indiana, took command of Davis's brigade and eventually resumed the advance. Precious time had been lost; that delay permitted the surprised Laurel Brigade time to organize and respond. The Federals were in danger of losing the initiative. Brigadier General John Buford wrote of Davis's loss:

> The success was dearly bought, for among the noble and brave ones who fell was Col. B. F. Davis, 8th N.Y. Cav. He died in the front giving examples of heroism and courage to all who were to follow. He was a thorough soldier, free from politics and intrigue, a patriot in its true sense, an ornament to his country and a bright star in his profession. When the sad news of Davis's fall reached me, I crossed and pushed to the front to examine the country and to find out how matters stood. I then threw the 1st Division on the left of the road leading to Brandy Station with its left extending toward the R[ail] Road.

Joe McKinney had this to say:

> With the death of Davis, the Union attack stalled. What could Buford have done, if anything, to regain momentum?[34] Did the senior officers left in the 8th IL and 8th NY (or Major McClure, the ranking officer in the brigade) know the mission and could one of them have taken charge?[35] Major Flournoy reacted quickly and moved to the sound of the guns. He was able to react quickly and adjust faster than Federals, particularly after the death of Grimes Davis.[36]

Note: Hart placed two guns on the Beverly Ford Road to delay the Federal advance. They fell back, alternating the guns as they went, to Saint James Church. From the traffic circle, looking north, you can see the slight knoll on which Hart placed his artillery.

View of Beckham's artillery park. Beyond the distant trees lies Beverly Ford. (Author's "photo" vice Authors "collection")

Captain Hart and his battery guidon, South Carolina Military Museum

The map below shows the advance of the Federal Cavalry past Captain Gibson's picket line location. The response of the 6th and 7th Virginia with the forming of the Confederate line near Saint James Church with Stuart's headquarters atop Fleetwood Hill.

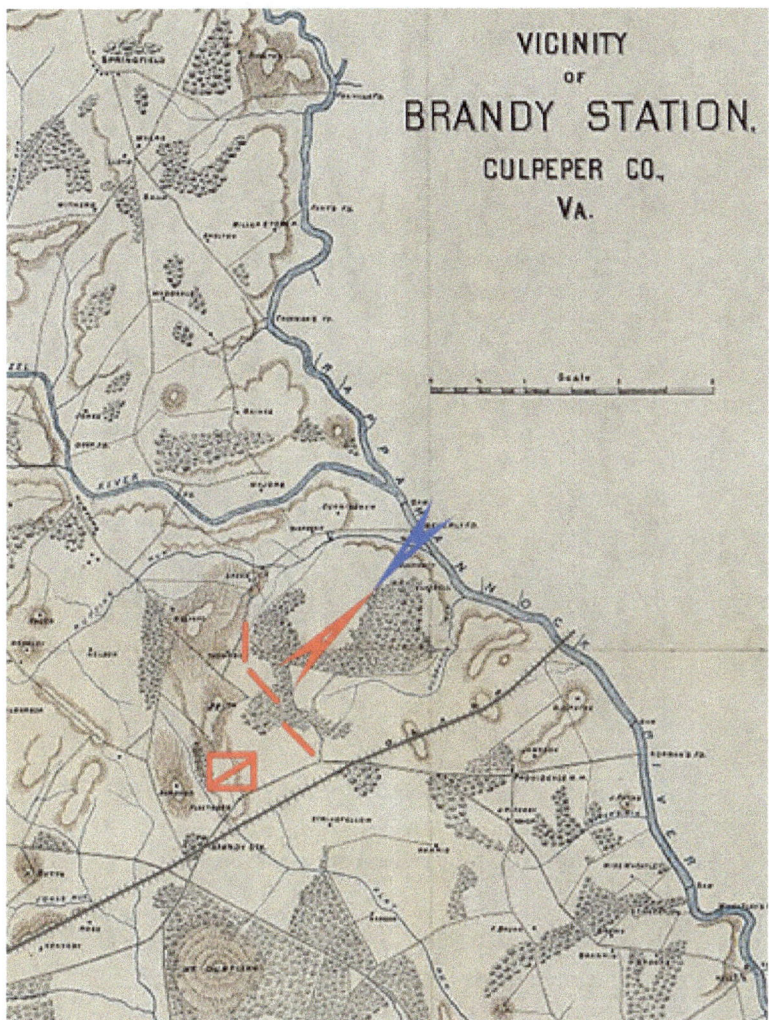

Map from Library of Congress, William W. Blackford, Graphics by author

       Your next stop will be Major Robert Beckham's new position near Saint James Church. Exit the parking lot and drive south about ¾ of a mile and turn right onto Saint James Church Road. Make an immediate left into the American Battlefield Trust parking circle. Exit your vehicle and walk across Saint James Church Road to the grassy area just off the road. You will be facing back toward the direction of the previous stop, northeast.

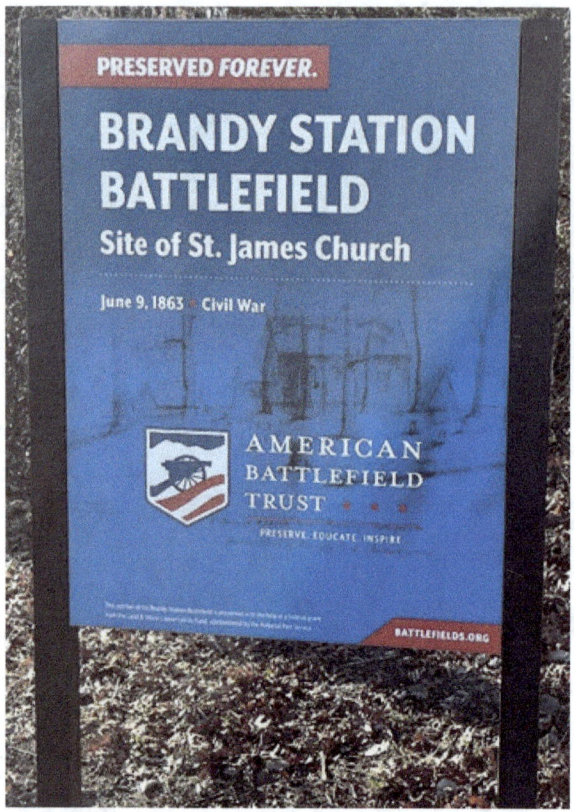

Saint James Church Parking area sign.
(Author's "photo" vice Authors "collection")

Stop 5 – Saint James Church – American Battlefield Trust parking lot

Orientation: North is off to your front left. Beverly Ford is about two miles north of your current position. Fleetwood Heights is just over a mile to the southwest. In 1863, the ground in front of you would have been devoid of trees for approximately 800 yards. This is the location of the Laurel Brigade's camp on 8 June 1863. Captain Beckham's horse artillery has displaced from the camp south of Beverly Ford and is now positioned along the ridge to your front extending from the Mary Gee House on right with Harts Battery, with Mormon's Battery next, McGregor's and Chews Battery on the knoll down to Saint James Church on your left.[37]

View looking back towards the direction of the Federal advance.
(Author's "photo" vice Authors "collection")

View showing location of Mary Emily Gee House and
the Headquarters of the 6th Virginia Cavalry on hill.
(Author's "photo" vice Authors "collection")

As the fighting shifted to the Saint James Church area, Pleasonton, the overall commander of the attacking Federal force, still had not reached the battlefield, He was relying on reports only, and at 0600 sent a dispatch to Hooker: "Enemy has opened with artillery and shows some force of cavalry. Col. Davis, commanding Second Brigade, First Division, led his column across and was gravely wounded." It is apparent that Pleasonton did not have a good situational awareness of the ongoing fight. Clearly at this point, Brigadier General John Buford was leading the fight for the Federals.

(Left) Brigadier General John Buford, commander, 1st Cavalry Division, Library of Congress

Brigadier General "Grumble" Jones busied himself setting in place his regiments to support Beckham's line of horse artillery near Saint James Church. Jones was still without his coat and boots on as he had not had the time to put them on. The 6th and 7th Regiments were disorganized and falling back to the area of the Gee House. Jones ordered the 11th and 12th Virginia along with the 35th Battalion to firm up the battleline centered around St. James Church and Beckham's guns. The 11th was ordered to dismount and advance through the woods on the left flank of Beckham's guns. The 35th and 12th initially remained mounted and in reserve behind the guns of the horse artillery. Jones decided he needed to "develop" the situation and ordered Asher Harmon's 12th Virginia cavalry forward. As the 12th advanced across the field as mounted skirmishers, unseen Federal troopers opened with accurate carbine fire. Harmon redirected some of his men to face the threat, and a hot fight developed at the edge of the wooded line opposite Beckhams guns.

Major Robert Morris Jr., of the 6th Pennsylvania Cavalry, under orders from Buford to attack, decided now was the time to charge the 12th Virginia. At around 0800, five companies of the 6th Pennsylvania, with elements of the 6th U.S. Cavalry in support, stepped out from the tree line.

The attack started off disorganized, as the 6th Pennsylvania came out of the woods piecemeal. The Pennsylvanians charged across the field toward the 12th Virginia and Beckham's guns. The 12th was thrown back in disorder. One member of Company H of the 12th Virginia stated: "It was then warm work, hand to hand, shooting and cutting each other in desperate fury, all mixed through one another, killing, wounding, and taking prisoners promiscuously." This stalemate lasted a while, with each charge being met by a countercharge.

Even when the 12th Virginia finally fell back, the 6th Pennsylvania encountered trouble from unseen drainage ditches. This slowed the attack and forced the Pennsylvanians to bunch up as the troopers negotiated the obstacle. Morris was thrown from his horse into one of the ditches, leaving the attack leaderless.

Seeing an opportunity to break up the attack, Jones ordered the 35th under "Lige" White to charge the Federal advance in the flank. The 6th Pennsylvania's attack reached its culminating point just shy of the horse artillery. The attack fell apart, and the Federals turned about and ran for their lives, suffering many casualties in the process. During the pursuit, the 6th U.S. Cavalry emerged from the woods and attempted to charge across the field, meeting the same results, and were pushed back by the 35th Battalion of Virginia Cavalry.

Joseph W. McKinney recalled of the Federal attack at Saint James Church, "This, to me, is an example of good concept but poor execution. The entire reserve brigade—five regiments—might have successfully penetrated Jones' line at St James, but the attack—delivered by only 1½ regiments—had no chance of success. One can fault Buford for giving the order w/o knowing the status of his forces."

Stuart arrived at Saint James Church about 0900. The Federal attack had stalled, and the Laurel Brigade was in control of the ground for the time being.

The map below shows the advance of the Federal Cavalry to Saint James Church. To the southeast, Beverly Robertson's Brigade encounters Brigadier General David Gregg's Federal cavalry at Kelly's Ford. To the southwest in Culpeper are elements of the Confederate Infantry.

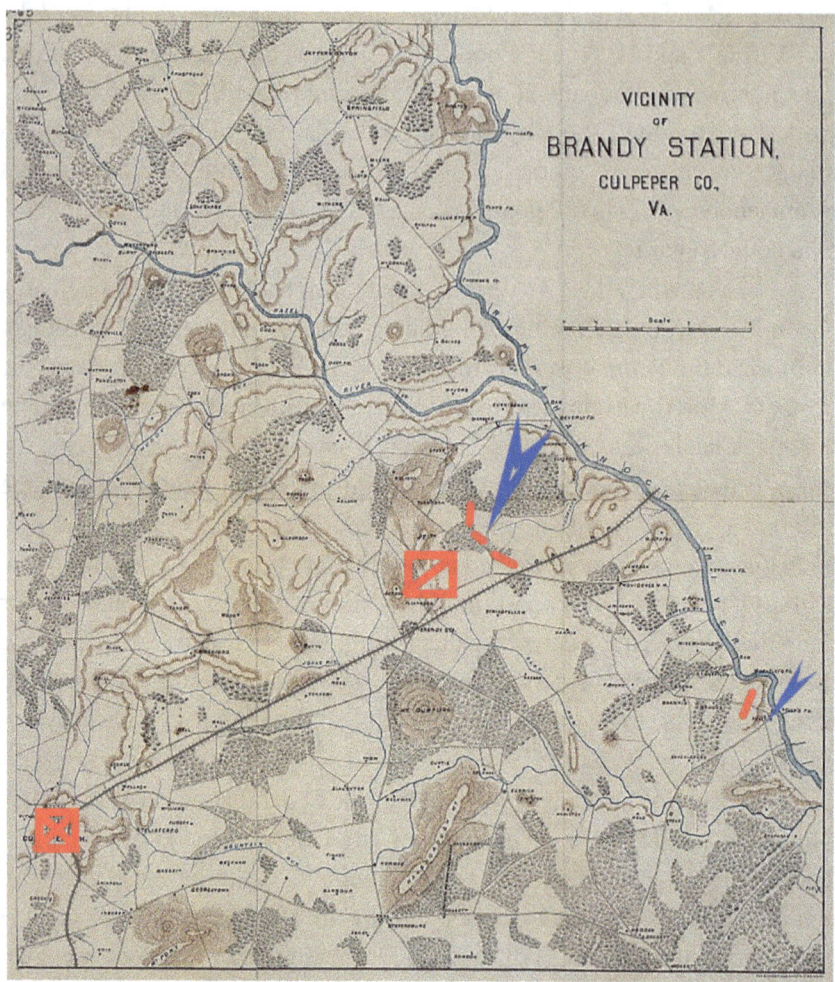

Map from Library of Congress, William W. Blackford, Graphics by author

     Return to your vehicle in the parking circle and turn right out of the parking area onto Saint James Church Road. At the stop sign, turn right onto Beverly Ford Road. Proceed a short distance and then bear right onto Cobb's Legion Road. At the stop sign, turn right onto Fleetwood Heights Road. About one mile up the road, you will notice the elevation starts to rise, at the peak of the high ground is the parking area for the next stop. Turn left into the American battlefield Trust parking lot. Use caution as you turn into the parking area as visibility for oncoming traffic is limited. Exit your vehicle and move toward the interpretive markers in the grassy area.

American battlefield Trust parking lot sign for Fleetwood Hill. (Author's "photo" vice Authors "collection")

Stop 6 –Fleetwood Heights – American Battlefield Trust parking lot

Orientation: As you exit your vehicle and walk toward the interpretive markers along the crest of the ridge to your front, you are facing South. North is in the direction back toward the parking lot. Off to your right (west) in the distance you can see the steeple of the church in Brandy Station. To your immediate front at the base of the hill is modern day Route 29 and just in front of that is the Orange and Alexandria railroad. Back over your left shoulder is the direction of Saint James Church and the previous stop from which you just left.

One of Stuart's staff officers, W. W. Blackford, left an account of the area around Fleetwood Heights:

> The waste of war had removed the obstacles to cavalry maneuvers usually met with in our country – fences and forests; and the ground was open, level and firm; conditions which led to the settlement of the affair with the sabre alone. Fleetwood hill was the key to the position. Artillery upon the commanding ground would render the surrounding plain untenable, and for its possession the battle was fought over its surface and on the levels beyond.

(Left) Captain William W. Blackford

Much work has been done by the American Battlefield Trust to purchase and restore Fleetwood Hill. Just a few short years ago the ground was privately owned with a large home and swimming pool, dominating the crest where Stuart's headquarters once stood. The ground just below the heights and over which the Federals attacked is preserved by the Brandy Station Foundation. This ground served as the location for the 100th and 150th anniversary ceremonies. See Appendix J for ceremony photos.

**View of Fleetwood Hill and interpretive markers.
(Author's "photo" vice Authors "collection")**

Miller House atop Fleetwood, 27 November 1863, Robert Knox Sneeden

View from Fleetwood Heights looking toward Brandy Station and the direction from which Percy Wyndham's Federal Cavalry Brigade attacked. (Author's "photo" vice Authors "collection")

At about 10:30 on 9 June 1863, the area around Stuart's headquarters was mostly bare. The tents had been struck, the baggage wagons sent to Culpeper for safety. General Stuart had ridden to St. James Church to direct the fighting. Only Major Henry B. McClellan and a few couriers remained behind to observe the field of battle and relay messages from the hilltop. The two regiments assigned to picket the high ground, the 4th Virginia and 2nd South Carolina, had been sent South to Stevensburg to protect the line of march to Culpeper to screen the infantry.

A courier from Robertson's command arrived to relay a message to Stuart's headquarters of another Federal advance from Kelly's Ford. While speaking with the courier, McClellan noticed off to the Southwest in the vicinity of Brandy Station railhead a large column of Federal cavalry approaching.

Other than a few miscellaneous staff officers and orderlies, the dominant topographical feature of the area lay unprotected. Fortunately, one artillery piece, a six-pounder Napoleon, of Captain Roger P. Chew's

Horse Artillery Battery, commanded by Lt. John W. Carter, happened to be there. Carter had exhausted his ammunition at St. James Church and had pulled back to Fleetwood to refill his limber. McClellan directed orderlies to inform Stuart, Jones, and Hampton of the situation. He ordered Carter to bring his gun forward, in view of the advancing Federals, and to open fire on them.

Stuart's headquarters flag, presented to the Richmond Library by Major Henry B. McClellan, American Civil War Center

McClellan described the scene:

> They were pressing steadily toward the railroad station, which must in a few moments be in their possession. How could they be prevented from also occupying Fleetwood Hill, the key to the whole position? Matters looked serious! But good results can sometimes be accomplished with the smallest means. Lieutenant Carter's howitzer was brought up, and boldly pushed beyond the crest of the hill; a few imperfect shells and some round shot were found in the limber chest; a slow fire was at once opened upon the marching column, and courier after courier was dispatched to General Stuart to inform him of the peril.

Carter's gun caused enough confusion among the advancing Federal cavalry that they halted their advance to get a better understanding of what might have been atop the heights.
McClellan continued:

> In point of fact there was not one man upon the hill beside those belonging to Carter's howitzer and myself, for I had sent away even my last courier, with an urgent appeal for speedy help. Could General Gregg have known the true state of affairs he would, of course, have sent forward a squadron to take possession; but appearances demanded a more serious attack, and while this was being organized three rifled guns were unlimbered, and a fierce cannonade was opened on the hill.[38]

McClellan's couriers found Stuart at St. James Church. As McClellan suspected might happen, Stuart was in disbelief that a federal column was behind his lines. However, the sound of Lt. Carter's cannon in the distance prompted Stuart to send the 12th Virginia and the 35th Battalion to Fleetwood.

> I think this is a good example of effective tactical command. Stuart positioned himself where he could see the fighting atop Fleetwood and see Jones' and Hampton's regiments advancing from the Saint James line. Stuart wasn't bashful about sending orders directly to regimental commanders (although Hampton took great umbrage). – Col. Joseph W. McKinney

McClellan met the lead elements of Harmon's 12th Virginia and urged them forward. As the 12th Virginia reached Fleetwood, Carter's withdrawing gun passed them heading in the opposite direction. Fleetwood was vacant of any Confederate troops.

As Captain William W. Blackford, of Stuart's staff, recorded: "There now followed a passage of arms filled with romantic interest and splendor to a degree unequaled by anything our war produced." Harmon, not pausing to organize the charge, advanced with the 12th in a column of fours right up the heights of Fleetwood. The 12th Virginia collided with the 1st Maryland on the crest of the hill starting some of the most savage combat of the war. Lt. Colonel "Lige" White briefly paused his battalion and aligned them for the charge. He then led his men atop Fleetwood Heights to join the fray that was underway. White and his men pushed past the Federal Cavalry and advanced down the east side of the hill overrunning the 6th New York artillery that had been brought up in support of the Federal attack.

The map below depicts the assault on Fleetwood Heights by Col. Percy Wyndham's cavalry brigade, and Stuart's reaction with elements of the Laurel Brigade.

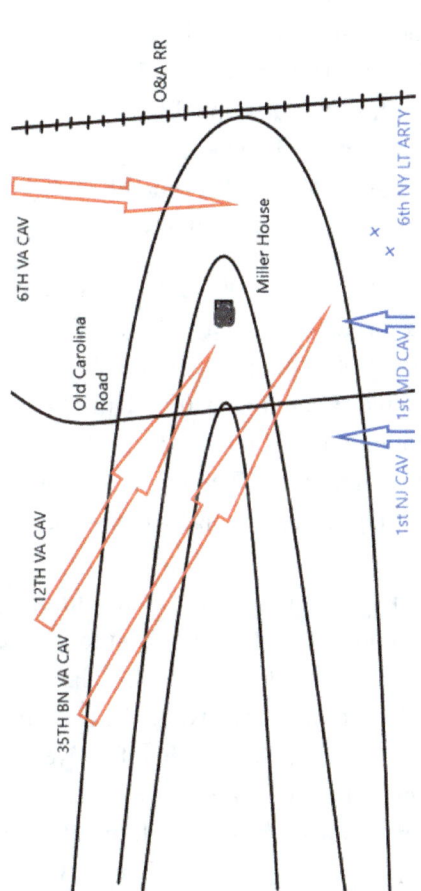

When the fight for Fleetwood commenced, Stuart ordered the rest of Jones's Brigade, and all of Hampton's Brigade, to ride to Fleetwood. Stuart himself displaced his command post and moved to Fleetwood as well. The fighting on Fleetwood was close and bloody. Clouds of dust swirled, adding to the confusion of the fight. The crest of the dominant hill changed hands numerous times. It was during this fighting that Harmon, commander of the 12th Virginia, was wounded by a saber slash to the back of the neck. Although seriously wounded and bleeding heavily, Harmon stayed on the field with his regiment. Major Cabell Flournoy and his 6th Virginia Cavalry were also ordered into the fight. Flournoy led his men south toward the O&A Railroad before advancing up the heights. This maneuver screened his advance and permitted Flournoy to charge onto the field into the flank of his opponent. Flournoy noted in his official report of the battle that his lone regiment charged into five regiments of Yankee cavalry as it joined the fray. Elements of the 6th Virginia, along with White's 35th, would again overrun the 6th New York Artillery.

The historian of the 35th Battalion (White's Comanches) noted:

> The gallant fellows at the battery hurled a perfect storm of grape upon the Comanches ... with never a halt or a falter the battalion dashed on, scattering the supports and capturing the battery after a desperate fight, in which the artillerymen fought like heroes, with small arms, long after their guns were silenced. There was no demand for a surrender, nor any offer to do so, until nearly all the men at the battery, with many of their horses, were killed and wounded. White and a few of his men attempted to turn Martin's guns on the Yankees, but White received no support, and a federal counterattack loomed. Prudently, White pulled back, leaving the guns for the Yankees.

It was likely during this encounter that White was wounded, although not seriously. Hampton's brigade arrived, along with the remainder of Jones's outfit. Leading from the front, Wade Hampton charged head on into the Federal cavalry on Fleetwood Hill. Stuart, following along behind Hampton's column, could be heard to yell: "Give them the sabre, boys!" The sight of the fighting on Fleetwood was one of utter chaos and confusion. Sabers flashing, pistols firing, screams of both men and horses resounded in the air.

According to an account by a 1st Pennsylvania Cavalry trooper, "At one time the dust was so thick we could not tell friend from foe." The regimental historian of the 10th New York Cavalry observed, "The rebel line that swept down on us came in splendid order, and when the two lines were about to close in, they opened a rapid fire upon us. Then followed an indescribable clashing and slashing, banging and yelling ... We were now so mixed up with the rebels that every man was fighting desperately to maintain the position the position until assistance could be brought forward."

Rallying his troopers, Federal Brigade Commander Colonel Kilpatrick shouted to the 1st Maine Cavalry: "Men of Maine! You must save the day! Follow me!" Kilpatrick personally led a charge of the Maine troopers. "In one solid mass this splendid regiment circled first to the right, and then moving in a straight line at a run struck the rebel columns in flank. The shock was terrific! Down went the rebels before this wild rush of maddened horses, men, biting sabres, and whistling balls." The charge of the 1st Maine saved the 6th New York artillery, which had been put near Fleetwood Hill.

Lt. J. Wade Wilson, commanding a federal battery, noted in his after-action report:

> I limbered to the front and sought a position on the crest of the hill behind which the enemy was rapidly massing to force back the advance of Col. Kilpatrick ... Before reaching the crest, however, a halt was ordered by Col. Kilpatrick, and, soon after, a retreat from that position, which was executed without panic and in admirable order. The enemy, perceiving the retreat, charged furiously up the hill and through the section fifty yards in rear of the pieces, charging desperately on the cavalry, some hundreds of yards in advance of the pieces in the retreat. The capture of the section seems to have thought accomplished by the enemy, and the rebel line wheeled into column and pushed rapidly by the flanks, with the intent to turn the right of the 1st brigade, leaving, as they supposed, a sufficient force to secure the guns. At this time was displayed the heroism of the section, and valor of which any command and country may be justly proud. In reversing, one of the gun limbers capsized, one wheel being in the air and the axle vertical. Perceiving this, I ordered the cannoneers to dismount and restore to its position the limber. We were surrounded by a squad of rebel cavalry, firing with carbine and pistol. The order

was scarcely needed, for the cannoneers had seen the peril of their gun, and, anticipating the order, had dismounted to restore it; and with revolvers in hand, they defended the gun as if determined to share its destiny and make its fate their own. The bearer of a rebel battle-flag was shot by Private Currant, who would have recovered it but for the great difficulty of approaching the color with a lame and skittish horse upon which he was at the time mounted. The flag was taken by the 1st Maine Cavalry.

As Captain Hart described the fight:

Scarcely had out artillery opened on the retreating enemy from this new position than a part of the 1st New Jersey Cavalry, which formed the extreme Federal left, came thundering down the narrow ridge, striking McGregor's and Hart's unsupported batteries in the flank, and riding through between guns and caissons from right to left, but met by a determined hand to hand contest from the cannoneers with pistols, sponge staffs, and whatever else came handy to fight with. Lieutenant-Colonel Broderick, commanding the regiment, was killed in this charge, as also the second in command, Major J. H. Shelmire, who fell from a pistol ball, while gallantly attempting to cut his way through these batteries. The charge was repulsed by the artillerists alone, not a solitary friendly trooper being within reach of us.

Nearing the end of the fight, Lunsford Lomax, leading the 11th Virginia Cavalry, arrived at Fleetwood Hill. They continued past the hill and once again, the men of the 6th New York Light Artillery were overrun. The artillerists spiked their three guns and left them on the field. The 11th Virginia continued their advance all the way to Brandy Station. Here, they drove the last of the Federal troopers from the town and secured Fleetwood from further attack. Your final stop for the staff ride will be at the Graffiti

House in Brandy Station. Return to your vehicle and make a left out of the parking area heading west onto Fleetwood Heights Road. Drive approximately two miles until you come to the stop sign with the commuter parking lot on your left. Turn left onto Alanthus Road and drive to the four-way light intersection on James Madison Highway. Drive across the intersection and turn left onto Brandy Road at the stop sign. Travel about 200 yards and go straight where the road bears to the right, staying on Brandy Road. Just ahead on the right is the Graffiti House. Pull into the parking lot.

Stop 7 – Graffiti House – Brandy Station Foundation parking lot

Orientation: This will be the final stop of the staff ride, the Brandy Station Foundation's Graffiti House visitor center and museum, at 19484 Brandy Road, Brandy Station, Virginia 22714. There are parking spots available to the right as you pull in. Picnic tables are provided under the shade trees just beyond the parking area. Restroom facilities and a small gift shop are available inside. Please call ahead of time to verify the hours of operation. https://www.brandystationfoundation.com/

Wartime view of Brandy Station and the Orange and Alexandria Railroad, Image Library of Congress

Modern day view of the well-preserved Graffiti House. (Author's "photo" vice Authors "collection")

The Brandy Station Foundation is a 501(c)3 non-profit organization dedicated to preserving the natural and historic resources of the Brandy Station area of Culpeper County, Virginia. The two-story frame house was built in 1858 by James Barbour. Barbour was a wealthy businessman whose home, "Beauregard," still stands about a mile and a half distant. It is likely the building was built for business use due to the proximity of the Orange and Alexandria Rail line and the main entrance's orientation toward the rail line. The building has served many purposes since its construction, including as a hospital on numerous occasions. It was purchased by the Brandy Station Foundation in August 2002 and opened to the public after extensive restoration efforts. Today visitors can see artifacts from the Civil War and preserved signatures and messages from both Federal and Confederate soldiers.

Saddlebag carried by Captain James Markham Marshall of Company E, 12th Virginia Cavalry. Item is on loan to the Graffiti House Museum by Robert Luddy.

Signature of Captain James Markham Marshall of E Company 12th Virginia Cavalry. The signature is on the second floor of the Graffiti House.

Signature of Michael Bowman

Signature of Sergeant Allen Bowman

Summary

With more than twenty thousand men involved, Brandy Station was the largest cavalry fight ever to occur in North America. The battle ended in a draw, although Stuart could claim victory as he held the field at the end of the day.

The Confederates sustained approximately 88 Killed/mortally wounded in Action and over 250 wounded plus another 225 missing in action." "The Federals suffered a combined total of 484 Killed/wounded and a reported 372 missing/prisoners. These casualties speak volumes for the severity of the fighting that day. The greatest consequence of Brandy Station was its positive effect on the morale of the Federal cavalry. Confederate staff officer Henry McClellan later wrote: "This battle ... made the Federal Cavalry. The fact is that up to 9 June 1863, the Confederate cavalry did have its own way ... and the record of their success becomes almost monotonous ... But after that time we held our ground only by hard fighting."

John N. Opie of the 6th Virginia Cavalry, noted:

> In this battle the Federal cavalry fought with great gallantry, and ... they exhibited marked and wonderful improvement in skill, confidence, and tenacity." One member of the 8th Illinois wrote to his parents two days after the battle: They had five brigades of cavalry, ten pieces of artillery, and Longstreet's infantry there. It was their intention to make raids on Maryland and Pennsylvania. We spoiled their fun anyway. We had about 10,000 cavalry and two 6-gun batteries and had 6,000 infantry ... Our object was accomplished. We had found out their strength and their intentions. They would have commenced crossing the river in an hour if we had not got the start of them.

The question as to who won the fight at Brandy Station will be one that will be discussed, or even argued, for years to come. Upon speaking with Joe McKinney, former President of The Brandy Station Foundation, back in 2014, I asked him for his thoughts were on the subject:

The question I always come back to is: Once the fight for Fleetwood began at about 10:30, why did Buford continue to draw forces from the main effort of the corps (destroying J.E.B. Stuart's division) to a secondary effort that had become unnecessary (turning Stuart out of his positions at St. James). Pleasonton and Devin saw Hampton's and Jones's regiments withdrawing from St. James? They could also see the fighting in Fleetwood (Pleasonton was near the Gee house). Buford may have not been able to see the fighting from the Cunningham farm, but he could certainly hear the artillery fire from the hill. The obvious Federal response to Gregg's attack would be to push forward to destroy Hampton and Jones. Why didn't Pleasonton order it?

Too often today we see commanders making the fatal error of falling in love with their plan. Did Pleasonton or Buford become fixated on the plan?[39]

No one can deny the success of the Federals in delaying General Lee's offensive operation. Lee waited through much of the following day, 10 June, to ascertain Hooker's intentions. When no further attacks came and no movement of any consequence was detected, Lee ordered Corps commander General Richard Ewell to march his men northeast from Culpeper late that afternoon toward the Shenandoah Valley.

Total casualties for the Laurel Brigade for the fight at Brandy Station included 27 killed, 9 mortally wounded, 112 wounded, and 122 missing for a total of 270 casualties or just over 13% of Jones's Brigade:

Unit	Killed	mortally wounded	wounded	missing	total
6th Virginia Cavalry	6	6	11	29	52
7th Virginia Cavalry	2	2	18	2	24
11th Virginia Cavalry	5	-	13	4	22
12th Virginia Cavalry	6	1	31	21	59
35th Battalion Virginia Cavalry	8	-	39	66	113

Chapter 5

Reflection

With every staff ride, there comes a time for reflection once the battle itself has been studied. It is appropriate to address the fates of some of the participants of the Battle of Brandy Station. Some of the Laurel Brigade soldiers remain on the battlefield in unmarked graves.

Brigade and Regimental Commanders

The commander of the Laurel Brigade, Brigadier General William E. "Grumble" Jones, survived the fight at Brandy Station and continued to lead cavalry troops for another year. In June 1864, Jones personally led an attack near Piedmont, Virginia. Accounts stated that he was swearing loudly as he led the charge of mounted troopers. Jones was fatally shot in the forehead in this charge, dying instantly. His grave is in Old Glade Spring Presbyterian Cemetery in Glade Spring, Virginia.

Grave of Brigadier General William E. Jones.
(Author's "photo" vice Authors "collection")

Major Cabell Flournoy, commander of the 6th Virginia Cavalry, can be called the savior of the morning for 9 June 1863. Through his heroic actions leading his men in the pre-dawn hours, and being in the thick of the fight for most of the day, Flournoy was not asked to step down from command of the 6th Virginia by the board of officers as they had ordered just prior to the battle. General Stuart would observe Flournoy in action at Rapidan Station leading a charge described as "the most brilliant charge of the war."[40] Stuart would follow up by recommending Major Flournoy to for promotion to Colonel for "extraordinary valor and skill." Colonel Harrison returned to the regiment shortly thereafter to resume command, but was wounded a month later and again left the regiment to Flournoy, who was struck down by enemy fire at Cold Harbor on 31 May 1864. The *Richmond Daily Dispatch* reported Flournoy's death on 2 June: "A cavalry fight occurred on Tuesday evening near Cold Harbor, in which Major Cabell Flournoy, commanding the 6th Virginia Cavalry, lost his life. His remains were brought in yesterday and forwarded to his home in Pittsylvania County." Flournoy is believed to be buried in an unmarked grave in Halifax. In 1841 the Flournoys purchased what is now the back part of Seven Oaks on Mountain Road in Halifax. There are no stones, only boxwoods, to mark the grave sites.

Virginia historic marker placed near the location of Major Flournoys death. (Author's "photo" vice Authors "collection")

Lieutenant Colonel Thomas Marshall led the 7th Virginia Cavalry in some of the most heated fighting of the day. Following the Gettysburg campaign, he was wounded twice, first at Ream's Station and second at Petersburg. He had multiple horses shot out from under him during his service. He was killed at Nineveh, in the Shenandoah Valley, on 10 November 1864. Two years after Marshall's death, in 1866, he was reinterred at the Stonewall Confederate Cemetery in Winchester, Virginia. Today, the cemetery is called Mount Hebron Cemetery. Marshall was laid to rest next the grave General Turner Ashby, former commander of the 7th Virginia Cavalry.

(Author's "photo" vice Authors "collection")

Colonel Lunsford Lomax would lead his regiment into some of the thickest fighting of the day at Brandy Station. He led the 11th Virginia through the remainder of the Gettysburg campaign and was promoted to

Brigadier General and transferred to Major General Fitzhugh Lee's Cavalry Division in September. He performed well in the overland campaign and was promoted to Major General in August 1864. Lomax commanded the cavalry division in Jubal Early's Army of the Valley. In March 1865, Lomax was put in command of the Shenandoah Valley and remained there until the end of the war a few weeks later. After the war, Lomax married and moved to Warrenton, Virginia to farm. In 1889, he became President of Virginia Polytechnic Institute and also worked for the War Department and served as commissioner of Gettysburg National Military Park. Lomax did in 1913 at the age of 77. He is buried in Warrenton.

(Author's "photo" vice Authors "collection"). Note that Lomax's first and middle name are reversed on his tombstone.

As noted, Colonel Asher W. Harman was wounded in the fighting on Fleetwood Hill, taking a saber wound to the neck but remaining in the fight until the matter was concluded. He returned to the 12th Virginia after his wound healed but only served briefly. While conducting a scouting mission near Bolivar Heights on 14 July, his small party of seven men was surrounded by a force of Federal cavalry. While attempting to flee, Harman's horse fell and he was captured. Harman remained a prisoner of war until February 1865 but did not return to active duty. After the war he returned to the railroad business with his brothers in Staunton, Virginia. He died in 1895 and is buried in Thornrose Cemetery, Staunton.

(Left) (Author's "photo" vice Authors "collection")

Colonel Elijah V. White was wounded in the fighting at Brandy Station. His 35th Battalion suffered more casualties at Brandy Station than any other Confederate unit. White would continue to lead the 35th through remaining campaigns of the war. On 6 April 1865, he was placed in command of Dearing's Cavalry Brigade after its commander was fatally wounded and taken prisoner. The brigade consisted of the 7th Virginia, 11th Virginia, 12th Virginia, and White's 35th Battalion of Virginia Cavalry: the remnants of the famous Laurel Brigade from Brandy Station minus the 6th Virginia. Rather than surrender, White disbanded the Brigade and the 35th on the 10 April. After the war, he returned home to Loudon County served as sheriff from 1866 to 1870. He also dabbled in commerce and served for 15 years as President of Peoples National Bank. He was active in church and veterans' organizations. White died on 11 January 1907 and was buried in Union Cemetery, Leesburg, Virginia.

(Author's "photo" vice Authors "collection")

6th Virginia Cavalry

**Capt. Bruce Gibson, Co A,
Mount Hebron Cemetery Winchester, VA**

**Joseph Anderson, Co. A
Union Cemetery, Leesburg, VA**

James M. Wood, Co B
Sperryville, VA.

Martin L. Baggarly, Co. B
Flint Hill, VA.

William G. Rudasill, Co. B
Sperryville, VA.

William K. Rudasill, Co. B
Sperryville, VA.

James Matthews, Co. K
Union Cemetery, Leesburg, VA.

John H. Lewis, Co. K
Union Cemetery, Leesburg, VA.

Guidon of Co. B. (Reproduction)
Rappahannock County Historical Society, Washington, VA.
The original guidon is housed in the American Civil War Museum, Richmond, VA
The guidon was preserved though donations from B Co. descendants.

7th Virginia Cavalry

**Lt. William W. Buck
Prospect Hill Cemetery, Front Royal, VA**

**William A. Bowling, Co. E
Flint Hill, VA**

**William A. Churchill, Co. E
Prospect Hill Cemetery, Front Royal, VA**

**Regimental Flag, preserved in the American Civil War Museum,
Richmond, VA**

11th Virginia Cavalry

Capt. Hugh H McGuire, Co E
Mount Hebron Cemetery, Winchester, VA.

Lewis A. Wilson, Co. A
Rixeyville, VA

**Believed to be the 11 Virginia Cavalry Regimental Colors
Private collection.**

12th Virginia Cavalry

Capt. George Baylor, Co. B
Zion Episcopal Cemetery, Charlestown, WV

Capt. James M. Marshall, Co E
Marshall family cemetery, Front Royal, VA

Lt. Thomas Marshall, Co E
Marshall family cemetery, Front Royal, VA

Lt. James M. Marshall, Co. E
Leeds Cemetery, Markham, VA

George B. Timberlake, Co B
Mount Hebron Cemetery, Winchester, VA

Harry Timberlake, Co B
Mount Hebron Cemetery, Winchester, VA

Robert W. Baylor, Co. B
Zion Episcopal Cemetery, Charlestown, WV

Richard C. Baylor, Co. B
Zion Episcopal Cemetery, Charlestown, WV

George H. Williams, Co E
Massanutten Cemetery, Woodstock, VA
Note: "Cavalry" is misspelled on his marker

Alexander M. Earle, Co I
Prospect Hill Cemetery, Front Royal, VA

**Thomas M. Garber, Regimental Color Bearer
Thornrose Cemetery, Staunton, VA**

35th Battalion Virginia Cavalry

Henry C. McFarland, Co. A
Union Cemetery, Leesburg, VA

William H Horseman, Co. A
Union Cemetery, Leesburg, VA

William T. Ambrose. Co E
Union Cemetery, Leesburg, VA

Chew's Battery

Capt. (Lt Colonel) Robert P. Chew. Commanding Chew's Battery
Zion Episcopal Church, Charlestown, West Virginia

Cpl. George M. Neese, Chew's Battery
Zirkle Cemetery, New Market, VA

John W. Henry, Chew's Battery
Killed in Action at Upperville
"He was shot through the head by a sharpshooter."

The Laurel Brigade fought in the Gettysburg Campaign and throughout the rest of the war. The 6th Virginia transferred to another brigade and the organization would change with multiple commanders over the remaining 22 months of war. During the last four days of its existence, Lt. Colonel Elijah V. White, commander of the 35th Battalion of Virginia Cavalry served as the Laurel Brigade's final commander. His final words to the brigade were retained by one of his men and published in the *Montgomery County Sentinel* of Rockville, Maryland:

> In the absence or orders from the Major General commanding I deem it my duty to you to declare the brigade disbanded and the members there at liberty to pursue what course your judgement dictates as right and honorable under existing circumstances. Your special conditions are so varied I cannot venture to advise you but believe me that whatsoever you may do or wherever you may go bear with you the best respects and confidence of him who has had the honor to command the gallant men of Ashby's old brigade. Allow me to thank you for the cheerful obedience you gave my orders and for the gallant achievements you won while under my command. Soldiers, you have done your duty and did it to the last. God bless you, Farewell.
>
> E.V. White, Lieutenant Colonel commanding brigade

Appendix A

Order of Battle, Laurel Brigade 9 June 1863

Brigade Commander - Brigadier General William E. "Grumble" Jones
6th Virginia Cavalry Regiment – Major Cabell E. Flournoy – 600 men*
7th Virginia Cavalry Regiment – Lt. Colonel Thomas Marshall – 400 men*
11th Virginia Cavalry Regiment – Colonel Lunsford L. Lomax – 400 men*
12th Virginia Cavalry Regiment - Colonel Asher W. Harmon – 290 men*
35th Battalion, Virginia Cavalry – Lt. Colonel Elijah V. White – 330 men*

* Approximately 2,020 men, sources vary on effective numbers.

Order of Battle, Stuart Horse Artillery Battalion 9 June 1863(5)

Battalion Commander - Major Robert F Beckham

Breathed's Maryland Battery (1st Stuart Horse Artillery) Captain James Breathed
-Four 3" Ord Rifles (1) (two 12-pound Napoleons?) (2) (Whitworth?) (3)

McGregor's Virginia Battery (2nd Stuart Horse Artillery) Captain William M. McGregor
-Two Napoleons, two 3" Ord Rifles

Chew's Virginia Battery (The Ashby Artillery) Captain Robert Preston Chew
- One British Blakely 12-pound rifled gun, One 12-pound howitzer, Two 3" Ord rifles
(6-pound Napoleon commanded by Lt. John Carter noted in reports)

Moorman's Virginia Battery (The Lynchburg Artillery or Beauregard Rifles). Captain Marcellus Moorman
-Two 10-pound Parrots, one 6-pound SB (Sept 62 report)? Converted to horse arty Oct 62

Hart's South Carolina Artillery (The Washington Artillery), Captain James F. Hart

-4 British Blakely 12-pound rifled guns

18 officers 519 men present for duty, 20 or 22 guns (4)

1. Maryland Scroll at Graffiti House identifies 16 crewmen from rifled gun #1
2. Brandy Station 1863 Dan Beattie page 50
3. According to Munford, the battery had a Whitworth with the section that supported Fitzhugh Lee's Brigade
4. Fighting with Stuart, David P. Bridges
5. Report of Major R. F. Beckham, C. S. Army, commanding Horse Artillery, of engagement at Brandy Station.

Appendix B

Report by Brigadier General W. E. Jones, Commanding Laurel Brigade

HEADQUARTERS JONES'S CAVALRY BRIGADE,
Brandy Station, Va., June 11, 1863.

MAJOR: I have the honor to enclose the reports of the commanders of troops under me on the 9th instant, in the battle near this place, and submit such remarks as seem pertinent to the occasion. At daylight, the report of small arms in the direction of Beverly Ford indicated a serious attack. Knowing the park of division artillery was without other protection than the pickets in front, its safety was doubtful. The Sixth Virginia Cavalry was on picket at the time, and the Seventh Virginia Cavalry was grand guard. Going to the scene of action at the top of speed, the Sixth and Seventh Regiments were found rapidly approaching the position of the enemy, only a few hundred yards beyond the artillery. The batteries being neither ready for action nor movement, it was a matter of the utmost importance to gain time. Major Flournoy, in command of the Sixth, was ordered down Beverly Road and to its right, and Lieutenant-Colonel Marshall on his left. Both were directed to attack with vigor whatever force they encountered. At the same time, directions were sent to the artillery to withdraw as quickly as practicable from the edge of the woods. The cavalry did its work well, but with considerable sacrifice. The artillery took position near the brick church. Captain W. K. Martin, assistant adjutant-general, having ordered up the Eleventh and Twelfth Regiments and Thirty-fifth Battalion Virginia Cavalry, they were posted in support of the artillery. When the Sixth and Seventh Regiments could no longer withstand superior numbers of footmen in the woods, they retired to the right and left of the position held by the remainder of the brigade. By this time, the enemy had penetrated through the woods, showing himself in some force in the open ground. A little shelling having caused a withdrawal, an attack was deemed expedient. Colonel Harman, leading with his regiment, moved along the road, supported on the left by the Thirty-fifth Battalion and Eleventh Regiment. As the head of Colonel Harman's regiment reached the woods, it received a severe fire, and was immediately charged by cavalry. The prompt arrival of support soon turned the tide of battle in our favor. The enemy lost here very considerably in killed and wounded and heavily in prisoners. About this time, General Hampton took position on my right, and General W. H. F. Lee notified me he was on my left. He was requested to keep up connection with me, which for some time was done, our lines making a right angle at the junction. The enemy now made his appearance in our rear, at Brandy Station and Miller's house. This was the force which early in the day was reported on by Captain [D. A.] Grimsley, through me to General Stuart, as advancing from Kellysville. Two regiments having been called for to meet this force of the enemy, the Twelfth Regiment and Thirty-fifth Battalion were sent, and the Sixth Regiment soon followed in support. General Hampton having withdrawn to the east side of the railroad, this part of the field was left in my charge with only a section of artillery and one regiment of cavalry [the Eleventh], the Seventh Regiment being then well to the left, more in connection with General Lee than with myself. My position becoming isolated and my force inadequate, I had started to make closer connection with General Lee, on my left, with the view of extending his line to join our forces with those near Brandy Station and Miller's house. The artillery was moved on the Jeffersonton road, to secure the heights between Barbour's and Thompson's houses. Orders coming now from General Stuart to move all my artillery and cavalry to Miller's house, the Eleventh Regiment was at once put in motion, and the artillery recalled to follow. The Seventh Regiment was ordered across the hills to the same point, and General Lee notified of the movement. I arrived in time to see the Twelfth and Sixth Regiments and the Thirty-fifth Battalion clearing Miller's hill of General Pleasonton's division of Federal cavalry. This charge was followed by the Eleventh, under Colonel Lomax. In this he captured the third and last time a battery of three pieces, the Sixth Regiment and Thirty-fifth Battalion having done so before him. Pushing his success, he divided his regiment, sending Captain [E. H.] McDonald with a squadron of his regiment, he assailed three regiments of cavalry awaiting him near the depot. He routed this whole force completely. Having driven them off, he sent, by order of General Stuart, two hundred men to Culpeper Court-House, and went himself with the remainder of his command to guard against another attack from the direction of Stevensburg. The Twelfth, Sixth, and Seventh Regiments were from this time on held in reserve, alternately supporting the artillery at Miller's house and re-enforcing General Lee, on our extreme left. The serious fighting being over, the brigade took no further active part. It resumed its picket posts by nightfall. My brigade bore the brunt of the action both in the morning and evening, and lost severely in killed and wounded, but had the satisfaction of seeing the enemy worsted in every more than ourselves. We ended the fight with more horses and more and better small arms than we had in the beginning. We took two regimental colors, many guidons, and a battery of three pieces. We took many prisoners, probably 250, as one regiment reports 122. Throughout the officers and men sustained their well-earned reputation for gallantry. To my personal staff I am under the greatest obligations. Lieutenant W. M. Hopkins entered the fight in the morning, killing his man in the charge near the brick church. Very respectfully, your obedient servant,

W. E. JONES,

Brigadier-General, Commanding.

Major H. B. McClellan,

Assistant Adjutant-General, Cavalry Division.

[P. S.] - List of killed and wounded: Killed 12, and wounded, 90. This is exclusive of the casualties of the Thirty-fifth Battalion and will in all amounts to 130 killed and wounded. The missing of prisoners cannot yet be ascertained, as some have straggled. The number of prisoners is known to be small.

HEADQUARTERS JONES' BRIGADE, June 11, 1863.

MAJOR: In addition to the property captured on 9th instant, already reported, I must report the capture of 20 horses by the Seventh Regiment Virginia Cavalry, under Lieutenant Colonel Thomas Marshall.

Very respectfully,

W. E. JONES,

Brigadier-General, Commanding.

Appendix C

Report of Major Cabell Flournoy, Sixth Virginia Cavalry

June 10, 1863.

CAPTAIN: In accordance with orders from brigade headquarters, I have the honor herewith to transmit the report of the part taken by my regiment in the battle of the 9th instant. Early in the morning, I was aroused by a couriers from Captain [Bruce] Gibson, Company A, announcing that the enemy had crossed the river in considerable force, and charged his post. He fought them gallantly for some minutes, charging and driving back their advance of 100 men, when they were stoutly re-enforced by two regiments of cavalry, and then they drove his pickets to within 300 yards of my camp. I hastily collected a portion of my regiment, amounting to about 150 men, and charged down the road toward Beverly Ford. Here I attacked two regiments of cavalry (the Eight New York and Eighth Illinois). We drove them before us for a short distance, killing and wounding some of them, and capturing 3 or 4 prisoners, with their horses, The prisoners mention Colonel Davis, of the Eighth New York, as killed. I wish to mention as acting with distinguished gallantry Lieutenant R. O. Allen and Lieutenant [C. G.] Shumate, of Company D. These officers led their men with distinguished gallantry. Lieutenant Shumate was severely wounded, but remained on the field all day, notwithstanding his left arm was entirely disabled. In this fight, Captains [D. T.] Richards and [William T.] Mitchell led their men well, and Sergeant [John B.] Stone, of Company H, acted very gallantly, killing 1 and capturing 2 of the enemy. He was afterward killed, fighting gallantly in the charge near the Miller house. Lieutenants [C. B.] Brown and [J. T.] Mann, of Company I, were killed while leading their men. Captain [J. A.] Throckmorton led the second squadron in fine style, charging to the right of the enemy's line; and although they proved too strong for him, he contested his ground fiercely, keeping them back for some time. The regiment held the enemy in check long enough for the baggage trains of the camps, which were nearby, to be gotten out of danger and the battery to be placed in position. In this position, I lost 30 men killed, wounded, and prisoners. My regiment was then ordered by General Jones to the right, where reported to General Hampton, and acted with his brigade. I was there ordered by him to move quickly in the direction of Brandy Station, and, while on my way, I received orders from General Stuart to cut off 300 Yankees who were near the Miller house. I moved across the railroad, and, instead of 300, I met what prisoners reported as five regiments. I charged with my regiment, now reduced by casualties and the detachment of four of my companies to 200 men. We drove back the whole force, and had them in retreat, when we were attacked in rear, and forced to fall back toward the Miller house, where the enemy opened on us with artillery. We charged, and took the battery, but were unable to hold it, having been charged by five times our number. We fell back in confusion toward the hill in front of the Miller house, where the men were rallied and reformed. Captain [R. H.] Owen, Company G, and Captain Mitchell, Company E, acted well in this fight, leading a squadron to the charge, which would have proved entirely successful had the enemy been kept off our rear. The officers and men of the regiment fought bravely until almost surrounded. We lost 24 men in this charge. Lieutenant Allen, Company D, was severely wounded while leading his men over the battery. I had 5 men killed, 25 wounded, and 24 taken prisoners (many of whom were wounded) in the two engagements. I am indebted to Surgeons [J. S.] Lewis and [Robert] Galt for their prompt and careful attention to my wounded.

      I am, captain, very respectfully, your obedient servant,
C. E. FLOURNOY,
Major, Commanding Sixth Virginia Cavalry.

Appendix D

Report of Lt. Colonel Thomas Marshall, Seventh Virginia Cavalry

June 10, 1863.

CAPTAIN: I herewith send a report of the part taken by the Seventh Regiment in the action of yesterday, in the vicinity of Beverly Ford and Brandy Station. Soon after reveille, a considerable skirmish fire in the direction of Beverly Ford showed that the enemy was making an advance. One regiment was mounted and moved at a rapid gait in a few moments to the scene of action. The reserve of the Sixth Regiment being immediately in our front, I ordered the Seventh to move upon our left flank, just as we were emerging from a skirt of woods, we came under the fire of the enemy's sharpshooters, protected by woods, about 200 yards distant. Not knowing what force might be hidden from view, we continued the charge upon the flank. The head of my column, which went some depth into the woods, fell back, encountering a superior force. At this point one of the enemy was killed and another taken prisoner, and about the same time 2 of our men were killed. I then received orders to fall back gradually, if pressed upon by a much heavier force. Throwing out skirmishers, I moved the regiment into a body of woods about 150 yards distant. Here several sharpshooters, in charge of Lieutenant [J. G.] Neff, were dismounted and placed near the edge of the woods, and protected by a fence, who kept the enemy in check. The pickets upon left having reported that the enemy had placed a piece of artillery in a position which would command the body of woods held by us, we fell back slowly, and, moving in the direction of Brandy Station, I drew up the regiment in line upon a commanding hill, with a wood in our rear, and from which position we had an extensive view of the field of battle. At this point, receiving orders to regain the position occupied earlier in the morning, the regiment was moved by me in column of fours in the direction of the river. Before this I had ordered out a body of sharpshooters, in charge of Major [S. B.] Myers, to feel the woods in our front, to ascertain the force of the enemy thought to have possession of it. Hearing from Lieutenant [W. W.] Buck, Company E, that there was a force of cavalry in such a position that we could gain something by an attack upon them, I ordered the regiment forward, and, as soon as we came in view, charged them. Before we came in effective range of them, they wheeled about, and made good speed. A portion of our column pursued them for some distance until they fell upon a supporting force. The enemy then opened upon us from a battery on our flank. I then moved the regiment into a column of fours under the shelter of a hill, at which point we fell in with General W. H. [F.] Lee's brigade, which had come up on our left. Being for the time effectually separated from our own brigade, I continued to operate in conjunction with General Lee. A portion of the artillery of the Third Brigade coming up, was placed in a commanding position, and did admirable service. We remained under the shelling of the enemy for some hours without any casualties, excepting a slight wound received by Captain [B. P.] Crampton from the bursting of one of the enemy's shells, as we were moving in the direction of Brandy, by order of General Lee. On my way, I received orders from General Jones to rejoin his brigade, which I did in a portion of the field about half a mile from brigade headquarters. Here we remained, resting in palace, until order to move up in column of squadrons, to charge the enemy in case of an attempt on his part to take our batteries. While in this position, the fighting on the left wing became much warmer, and the Seventh was ordered to go to the support of General W. H. [F.] Lee, at a rapid trot. Arriving near the scene of action, and upon information given by a soldier who knew the position of affairs, I ordered a charge; but upon reaching the brown of a very steep hill, our column was a good deal separated. Instead of finding the enemy at the point indicated, they were discovered drawn up in heavy force upon a still higher eminence and protected in their rear by some wood. In this charge, which resulted only in checking their advance, our right flank was fired upon by one of the enemy's batteries, and we had 1 man wounded. I then fell back, and, in accordance with an order from Colonel [J. L.] Davis (who was commanding in that portion of the field, General Lee having been wounded), I moved down in column of squadrons, preparatory to a charge upon the enemy. We were afterward ordered to support General Roberson, and subsequently, in the evening, to support infantry skirmishers. At the close of the day, we received orders to move in the direction of our old camp. Thence we marched in the direction of Beverly Ford and took charge of the picked posts in that vicinity. Our loss in killed, wounded, and missing is as follows: Killed, 2 men, 1 in Company C, and 1 in Company F; wounded, mortally, as supposed, 2 (1 since dead); severely, 4; slightly, 8; not seriously, 6. Total killed and wounded, 22. Among the wounded is Sergeant Whiting, who is represented to have acted with a great deal of gallantry.

    Very respectfully,
    THOMAS MARSHALL,
    Lieutenant-Colonel, Commanding Seventh Virginia Cavalry.
    Captain W. K. MARTIN,
    Assistant Adjutant-General.

[P. S.] There were also 2 men missing, supposed to be captured. Our loss in horses was – killed, 8; wounded, 15. Both officers and men acted their parts well, and though not on this occasion tested by any imminent peril, yet I feel quite sure they would have done their duty had such been the case. The report upon horses, arms, saddles, captured will be handed in by the adjutant of the regiment.

Appendix E

Report of Colonel Lunsford Lomax, Eleventh Virginia Cavalry

JUNE 9, 1863.

CAPTAIN: I beg leave to submit the following report of the part taken by this regiment in the late engagement: The regiment moved out about sunrise to the brick church on the road from Brandy Station to the river, where we remained formed in the woods until the enemy advanced from the woods in front, when we charged them, driving them back through the woods, killing and capturing several. In this charge, we passed a column of the enemy's cavalry charging our battery near the church. This was attacked by a squadron under Lieutenant-Colonel Funsten and repulsed with a slight loss on our side. The regiment was again formed in the woods, and the sharpshooters dismounted and dismounted and deployed in front, under Lieutenants [Joseph H.] Sherrard, Company H, and [William M.] Hockman, Company E. Both officers were severely wounded and brought to the rear, Lieutenant Hockman's wound proving fatal. I then moved the regiment to the support of a battery on our right, leaving the sharpshooters in front communicating with those of General W. H. F. Lee's brigade, on our left, but was ordered in a short time by the major-general commanding to attack the enemy's cavalry, now advancing from the right and rear of our present position. Moving rapidly in the direction of Brandy Station, I charged the enemy on the right of the Culpeper Court-House Road, and drove them across the railroad, capturing a battery of three guns and many prisoners. Observing a force of the enemy at Brandy Station, I moved toward that point, and found three regiments of cavalry, under Sir Perch Wyndham, plundering and destroying the property there. I charged, and drove them from the station, taking a stand of colors and many prisoners (among them a colonel), and pursued them some distance on the Stevensburg road. I was then ordered by the major-general commanding to advance upon Culpeper Court-House, and drive the enemy, reported to be there, from that point, and to place a picket on the Stevensburg road. I sent 200 men to Culpeper Court-House, and ascertained that no enemy had been there, and sent a squadron on the Stevensburg road. This squadron captured the enemy's picket of 14 men and sent in during the evening 20 men. Our loss during the day was 5 killed and 11 wounded. Among the first was Lieutenant Hockman, Company E; and of the wounded are Major [M. D.] Ball, and Lieutenant Sherrard, Company H. The regiment captured, as far as the company commander can ascertain, 122 prisoners. Our loss in prisoners is small; the exact number not known (but does not exceed 5 or 6), as missing men are still reporting. The return of the property captured by the regiment accompanies this report.* The universal good conduct of officers and men need not be commented upon by me, as they were acting under the eye of both brigade and division commanders.

    L. L. LOMAX,
    Colonel, Commanding Eleventh Virginia Cavalry.
    Captain W. K. MARTIN, A. A., Jones' Cavalry Brigade.

Appendix F

Report of Colonel Asher Harman, Twelfth Virginia Cavalry

JUNE 10, 1863.

GENERAL: In the engagement of yesterday, my regiment was engaged the whole day. In the morning, we were engaged on the Beverly Ford Road, at which point the enemy was repulsed, losing his colors and a good many prisoners. After this engagement, I was ordered with my regiment to move in the direction of Brandy Station. Before getting to the latter place, I encountered the enemy in large force, and failed in repulsing him until re-enforcements arrived. My sharpshooters were engaged during the remainder of the day. My loss in both officers and men was quite severe. The following is a list of the arms and horses captured on yesterday:

Colt's army pistols__ 68
Sharps rifle__ 40
Sabers __ 50
Horses __ 39

Very respectfully, your obedient servant,
A. W. HARMAN,
Colonel Twelfth Virginia Cavalry.
Brigadier General W. E. JONES, Commanding Jones's Brigade.

ADDENDA.

List of Casualties in the Twelfth Cavalry on the 9th instant.

Officers and Men	Killed	Wounded	Missing	Total
Company A				
Commissioned Officers		1		1
Enlisted Men		3	1	4
Company B				
Commissioned Officers			1	1
Noncommissioned Officers	1			1
Enlisted Men	2	4	2	8
Company C				
Noncommissioned Officers		1		1
Enlisted Men	1	3		4
Company D				
Enlisted Men		4	2	6
Company E				
Commissioned Officers		1		1
Noncommissioned Officers		2		2
Enlisted Men	2	1	1	4
Company F				
Enlisted Men		3	1	4
Company G				
Commissioned Officers		1		1
Noncommissioned Officers		1		1
Enlisted Men			1	1
Company H				
Commissioned Officers		1		1
Noncommissioned Officers			1	1
Enlisted Men		3	1	4
Company I				
Commissioned Officers		1		1
Enlisted Men		2		2
Company K				
Enlisted Men		2	2	4
TOTAL	6	34	13	53

T. B. MASSIE,

Lieutenant-Colonel, Commanding Twelfth Virginia Cavalry.
June 13, 1863.

*Nominal list omitted; Colonel A.W. Harmon wounded

Appendix G

Report of Lt. Colonel Elijah V. White, Thirty-Fifth Battalion

JUNE 10, 1863.

GENERAL: I have the honor herewith to send you a report of the part taken by the battalion (Thirty-fifth Virginia) which I commanded in the cavalry fight of Brandy Station, June 9. When it was known that the enemy was advancing, and we had been taken to the front to meet him, I was ordered by you to prepare to support the Twelfth Regiment (Colonel Harman's). I commenced immediately to form my men into line of battle. Before my line was completed, however, I was ordered to charge the column of the enemy. I called to my men, and they answered me with a cheerful and gallant spirit, not a man flinching from the stern duty that awaited him. We had not proceeded over 200 yards, when we were met by the Twelfth, retreating in disorder before the confident and fiercely pursuing enemy. Of course, the ranks of the squadron which I was leading in the charge were thrown into confusion, but this untoward circumstance checked us only for a moment. We continued our dash upon the enemy, driving him back before us over 100 yards, into the woods from which he had advanced. Here he was re-enforced, and we were compelled to fall back before his superior numbers, thus largely increased. I soon, however, succeeded in rallying my men, and we charged him over a half mile through the woods. At the edge of the woods, an officer, who was supposed from his uniform to be a general, was killed, while earnestly but vainly endeavoring to check the flight of his men. A major was captured by Private Sheehan, of Company B, after a fierce hand-to-hand conflict, in which he was severely handled. We captured and sent to the rear 25 commissioned officers and privates, among them a staff officer. I would here state-as probably some of the prisoners captured by my men were taken back by persons connected with other commands – that I ordered my men to turn over all prisoners as soon as they could find parties to take charge of them. While I was fighting the enemy in front, my squadron was charged in the rear by another considerable force, which was met and driven back in most gallant style by the squadron, which had been disordered by the broken ranks of the Twelfth and had thus been separated from me. While I can proudly boast of the coolness and stubborn courage displayed by all the men of the Thirty-fifth Battalion upon that occasion, I cannot in justice omit to call your particular attention to the conspicuous daring of First Lieutenant Joshua R. Crown, Company B. Ever in the front, dealing telling blows upon the vandal enemy, he elicited the warm admiration of all who beheld him, and infused his own chivalrous spirit into those who followed, thus proving a tower of strength to us and a stumbling-block to the foe. If ever a man deserved the reward of promotion for meritorious conduct, he did in the opening fight of the great battle of Brandy Station. About 1 o'clock, after it was known that the enemy had succeeded in flanking us, and had appeared in great force in our rear, I was ordered to join the Twelfth, and to support it in case of need. On arriving near the house which had been occupied by General Stuart as his headquarters, I was ordered by him to form my battalion in line of battle on the left of the road leading to Culpeper Court-House and charge the squadrons around the house. Here again I lost time and was thrown into some confusion by a squadron of the Twelfth, which broke through my line. My men were soon formed, however, and I ordered the first squadron, under the command of Captain [George M.] Ferneyhough, Company F, to charge the enemy occupying the grounds in front of the house – three squadrons – while I, with the two remaining squadrons, attacked a regiment to the left and in the rear of the house. Both charges were successful. We drove him from the hill, and down the road that led across the railroad. I had pursued the fleeing Federals about 200 yards, when I was informed that another regiment of the enemy had come up in my rear, cut off my first squadron, and retaken the hill from which he had just been driven. I ordered 20 men to continue the pursuit from which I was thus reluctantly forced to desist and returned with the remained of my command to renew the contest for the possession of the hill. The contest, though fierce, was soon decided. My brave followers rushed upon the force occupying it with the irresistible energy of men determined not to be conquered. It was soon broken and scattered, with the loss of its colonel, who was killed in the conflict. At this time, I was re-enforced by a company of the Sixth Virginia, and, with what men of my own I could collect and this company, I ordered a charge upon the battery that was stationed on the Culpeper Road, about 300 yards west of the crest of the hill where I then was. This battery had been playing upon me the whole time. Such a glorious charge as was then made by the gallant band that I shall ever be proud to have commanded on that occasion, I have not witnessed during this war. Through the terrible and destructive rain of grape and canister and leaden bullets poured upon them by the battery and the large cavalry force supporting it, it dashed fearlessly, fiercely on, until it swept like a whirlwind over the battery and into the ranks of the supporting force. It was soon scattered like chaff, and the battery was ours. How my heart swelled with pride then and there, when I thought of the power that nerves a freeman's arm when striking for his rights! The men at the battery fought with desperation, continuing to fire their small arms after they were surrounded. There was no demand for a surrender or offer of one until all the men, with many of their horses, were either killed or wounded. We were destined, however, to hold the battery but for a short time. I had no support sent to me, and, being entirely unprotected, I was soon surrounded by the enemy, who came down upon me from every quarter. All my men excepting about 20 were pursuing the cavalry that had supported the battery. The few left were involved in a difficulty from which it was all but impossible to extricate themselves; but the coolness and bravery which had led them to deeds of noblest heroism throughout that terrible day did not desert them now, and they cut their way through the thick, close ranks of the foe, though not without the loss of half their number. It would be difficult and invidious to call special attention to the conduct of any individual when all did their duty so well. I have never known men to act with more unshrinking gallantry than those of my battalion did throughout the day; not a man I saw or heard of failed to come up to the full requirements of the occasion. We captured in this battle four stand of colors, one of which was sent to Culpeper, one lost in the charge on the battery, and the other two I have in my possession. Private B. C.

Taylor, of Company C, while in full charge through a regiment, snatched the colors from their bearer, and carried them safely away. We captured also about 100 prisoners, a number of arms, horses, and equipment's, many of which we were compelled to turn over to different quartermasters and individuals, as I did not permit the men to encumber themselves while every man was needed to repel the foe. While I write this report with a just pride in the gallant Confederate soldiers whom I have the distinguished honor to command for shall be proud to command them, if I live, upon other fields, I deem it not unmanly to give a tear to the brave dead, who have sealed with their life-blood their devotion to their country and to the great cause of justice, truth, and liberty. The following is a list* of killed, wounded, and missing: Total killed, wounded, and missing, 90.

Respectfully submitted.

E. V. WHITE,

Lieutenant-Colonel, Commanding Thirty-fifth Battalion.

General W. E. JONES, Commanding

Appendix H

Report of Major R. F. Beckham, C. S. Army, commanding Horse Artillery, of engagement at Brandy Station.

JUNE 12, 1863.

MAJOR: I have the honor to report that, on the morning of June 9, four companies of the horse artillery were encamped on the Beverly Ford Road, about 1 1/2 miles from the river. The fifth company (Breathed's) had been detached, and was at this time higher up the river, with General W. H. F. Lee's command.

Just before sunrise, I received information to the effect that our pickets had been driven in, and that the enemy was advancing rapidly in large force. I immediately directed Captain [J. F.] Hart to place one piece by hand in the road and ordered all the others to be hitched up as promptly as possible, and to take position on the high ground, about 600 or 800 yards south of the camp.

The enemy approached rapidly and boldly, and had it not been for the delay of a few minutes caused by the arrival of a regiment under General Jones, it is more than probable we would have been compelled to abandon the pieces. As it was, several of the horses were wounded before we could move from camp.

The position first taken was just opposite Saint James Church, and on the east of the road. This was held with ease against the enemy's column for two hours or more, and could, I think, have been held all day had not the appearance of the enemy in our rear rendered it necessary to abandon this point, to regain Pettis' hill, which the enemy had occupied with his cavalry. In this first position taken up, three of the pieces had become disabled from the shock of the recoil; one had been detached with Colonel Butler, on the Stevensburg road; two were on the Kellysville road, and two had been placed, by order of the major-general commanding, on Pettis' hill. This left only five pieces (now exhausted of ammunition) within reach, to be brought into action. Three of these, by General Stuart's order, were left with General Jones, and the remaining two (McGregor's) were moved to the rear, to assist in driving the enemy from the position north of Brandy. Captain Hart also succeeded in getting into position one of the guns whose carriage had already been damaged, and fortunately succeeded in firing two or three highly effective shots before the carriage was completely disabled.

The pieces first placed on Pettis' hill were under the command of Lieutenant [John W.] Carter, of [R. P.] Chew's battery, and had been repeatedly charged by the enemy and retaken by our cavalry, and at the time that the two guns of McGregor's were brought toward the crest of the hill, it was very doubtful which party had possession of it. The two guns were, however, moved up rapidly, and scarcely had they reached the top, and before they could be put in position, a small party of the enemy charged them: The charge was met by the cannoneers of the pieces. Lieutenant [C. E.] Ford killed one of the enemy with his pistol; Lieutenant [William] Hoxton killed one, and Private Sully [Sudley?], of McGregor's battery, knocked one off his horse with a sponge-staff. Several of the party were taken prisoners by the men at the guns.

Fire was then opened from these guns on the enemy toward Brandy Station, and soon afterward I was enabled to get together the guns which had been sent on the Kellysville road, or left with General Jones, and to place them in position for clearing the plain about the hill. My guns were kept in position on this hill, firing slowly, until the enemy had recrossed the river, and I received an order to withdraw.

During all the morning, the firing had been quite regular, but not very rapid, and in the first position directed all the time at the skirmishers of the enemy and the masses concealed in the woods. I was not able to judge positively of the effect of the firing, owing to the covered ground the enemy occupied, he rarely showing more than his line of sharpshooters. However, I learn since that a large number of his horses were left dead in the woods and have no doubt that he suffered severely in men also. The little firing done in regaining Pettis' hill was perfectly accurate and powerful in its results, scattering the columns of the enemy advancing to the charge.

Captain Breathed, whose battery was with General W. H. F. Lee, in the vicinity of Freeman's, reports that about 8 a. m. of the 9th instant, one section, under Lieutenant [P. P.] Johnston, recrossed the Hazel River, and took position guarding the road leading from Beverly toward Welford's Ford; the other section was near Starke's Ford. The section under Lieutenant Johnston contended successfully with the enemy's sharpshooters and a battery of four guns, holding its position until ordered to retire, about 2 p. m. In retiring, it was joined by the other section, and ordered to take position at a point about 2 miles west of Brandy Station, whence a desultory fire was kept up on the enemy, who soon commenced retiring across the river.

The skill and good conduct of the men under Lieutenant Johnston have been highly extolled by cavalry officers who were present during the action, and much bloody evidences of the good effect of their work were left on the field in their front.

Privates Young, Wagner, and [T. D.] Loudenslager, whose good conduct is specially noticed, were wounded with their guns.

The reports of captured property have already been sent to the division quartermaster and ordnance officer.

The following constitute the casualties; Killed—Corporal [A. E.] Dornin, of Moorman's battery; wounded, 3 privates; missing 1. Wounded 1 of Hart's battery, 3 of Chew's battery, and 3 of Breathed's battery. Total—Killed, 1; wounded, 10; and missing, 1.

Respectfully submitted.

R. F. BECKHAM,

Major, Artillery.

Maj. H. B. MCCLELLAN,

Assistant Adjutant-General, Cavalry Division.

Appendix I

Report of Brigadier General John Buford, 1st Cavalry Division

Headquarters 1st Division and Cavalry Reserve
Near Warrenton Junction, Virginia
June 13th, 1863
Lieutenant Colonel A. L. Alexander
Acting Adjutant General Cavalry Corps
Colonel,

I have the honor to report as follows of the part taken by the troops under my command in the cavalry engagement on the 9th instant near Beverly's Ford.

In pursuance to instructions from the Brigadier General commanding the Corps, during the afternoon and night of the 8Lu instant I placed my command composed of the 1st Division, Reserve Brigade and [Brigadier] General [Adelbert] Ames' infantry, near to the ford unobserved by the enemy. About 4 AM the column was in motion, Colonel [Benjamin F.] Davis' 1st Brigade (8th Illinois, 3rd Indiana, 8th New York, 2 squadrons of 9th New York, and one squadron of 3rd [West] Virginia numbering 1,534 aggregate) leading.

At 4:30 AM the ford was taken, and the enemy's pickets driven to the woods, some five hundred yards from the river. As soon as Colonel Davis' force was across, I directed him to push the enemy for a mile or more. He started and in a very few moments became engaged with the enemy strongly posted in the woods and behind barricades. He nevertheless drove them from their stronghold, through the woods back upon their artillery, and held them there, although they made desperate efforts to recover their lost ground. This woods was dearly bought, for among the noble and brave ones who fell was Colonel B.

F. Davis, 8th New York Cavalry. He died in the front giving example of heroism and courage to all who were to follow. He was a thorough soldier, free from politics and intrigue. A patriot in the true sense, an ornament to his country and a bright star in his profession. When the sad news of Davis' fall reached me I crossed and pushed to the front to examine the country and to find out how matters stood. I then threw the 1st Division on the left of the road leading to Brandy Station with its left extending toward the railroad. General Ames' command was brought up and posted on each side of the road, in the skirt of the wood out of view, but facing and close to the enemy. The Reserve Brigade

(Composed 2nd, 5th, 6th United States Cavalry and 6th Pennsylvania Cavalry, the 1st United States being on picket) was posted on the right all connecting from right to left. While making this formation my extreme left was severely pressed by the enemy's skirmishers and artillery. Everything being arranged the Reserve under Major [Charles J.] Whiting swung around, gained the enemy's left flank and went at them, the 6th Pennsylvania Cavalry, under Major [Robert, Jr.] Morris leading, supported by the rest of the Brigade and [First Lieutenant Samuel S.] Elder's Battery [Horse Battery E, 4th US Artillery Regiment]. The Brigade was delayed in getting out of the woods and in the eagerness for the advance, the column became lengthened.

The 6th Pennsylvania, supported by a portion of the 6th US Cavalry, under Captain [George C.] Cram, when in reach, charged the enemy home, riding up to the mouth of his cannon. The 2nd US cavalry was to have followed, but before getting clear of the woods had received different orders.

This attack relieved my left which was sorely pressed and drew the enemy to my extreme right, where they massed, and threatened to overwhelm me.

Colonel [Josiah H.] Kellogg's Brigade [2nd Brigade, 1st Cavalry Division] (17th Pennsylvania and 6th New York) and a section of [Captain William M.]

Graham's Battery [Horse Battery K, 1st US Artillery Regiment] then took the extreme right, resting on Hazel Run. In this position there was very severe work for the skirmishers and artillery for several hours, at one time the enemy's dismounted men tried to gain a stone fence immediately in front of some of our guns. Captain [James E] Harrison, with a portion of his brave regiment [5th US], was sent to gain it first and to keep it. He did so in splendid style and for several long hours he held it and punished those who came in sight to oppose him. He remained long after his carbine ammunition was expended in a very awkward place, the dispositions of the troops being such I could get no relief for him. Finally, he was relieved but not until many of his horses were killed.

While in this position [Brigadier General David M.] Gregg's guns were heard and the enemy began moving. Major Whiting, with his Brigade and Elder's Battery, soon pressed forward driving the enemy over two miles up Hazel Run. Gregg's cannonading becoming more distinct and furious, I resolved to go to him if possible. All the forces with me except the 5th US Cavalry and a section of Graham's [Battery] which was left to hold my right, swung around under a tremendous artillery fire and gained the crest overlooking Brandy Station. Then came the [?]. A portion of the Reserve after much difficulty forced its way through a dense forest and became engaged after exhausting the little ammunition it had left, out flew the sabers and most handsomely were they used. The enemy, although vastly superior in numbers was fought hand to hand and was not allowed to gain an inch of ground once occupied. During this hand-to-hand fighting Lieutenant [Albert O.] Vincent [Horse Battery B and L, 2nd US Artillery Regiment] poured his shot into them with terrible execution. By this time Gregg's firing had ceased, and I was ordered to withdraw. Abundance of means was sent to aid me, and we came off the field in fine shape and at our convenience. Captain [Richard S. C.] Lord with the 1st US came up fresh, comparatively, with plenty of ammunition and entirely relieved my much exhausted but undaunted command in a most commendable style. The engagement lasted 14 hours. My loss I regret to report is heavy, annexed is a recapitulation. The enemy suffered equally.

General Ames' command behaved handsomely, and to him I am much indebted for his hearty cooperation, always given and with so much alacrity that his services were invaluable. I trust his loss is not as severe as mine. The men and officers of the entire command without exception behaved with great gallantry. Colonel [Thomas C.] Devin, who succeeded

Colonel Davis and fought the 1st Division deserves great praise. He was sorely pressed many times and most nobly did his brave men hold their ground. The Reserve Brigade was under my own observation all day and I had opportunity to see many acts of gallantry. All were conspicuous, but among so many brave, tried men it is difficult for me to say who excelled the others. Without doing injustice I may be allowed to say that Major Morris, 6th Pennsylvania, Captain Merritt and Harrison, at the head of their fighting regiments; [Second] Lieutenant [Andrew] Stoll [6th US] with his dashing squadron; and [First] Lieutenant [Thomas B.] Dewers [2nd US] with his gallant skirmishers, won my admiration.

Lieutenant Elder, Vincent and [Thomas, Jr.] Williams [Horse Battery E, 4th US Artillery Regiment] of the artillery, deserve great credit. They fought their guns with coolness, skill, and judgment and often where they were in hot places.

I transmit herewith the report of Colonels Devin and Kellogg and all the reports from the Reserve brigade. I fully endorse all they say of their officers and men and would mention more names, but for fear of doing someone injustice I must close.

To my staff, Captains [Myles W.] Keogh, [Theodore C.] Bacon; Lieutenants [John] Mix, [P.] Penn Gaskill and [William] Dean, I am under many obligations for their prompt and untiring exertions. I often had to send them where the fire was hot and when their horses were jaded, but there was no hesitation. Lieutenant Mix's horse was killed under him while delivering an order to a line of skirmishers. Captain

[Joseph] O'Keeffe early in the day obtained my consent to serve for Major Whiting, and late in the day while leading a charge of the 2nd US cavalry was wounded and taken prisoner. To Captains [Elon J.] Farnsworth, 8th Illinois, and [Ulric] Dahlgren, General Hooker's staff, I tender my thanks. To the former for the valuable information he gave me concerning the country, and enemy, and to the latter for volunteering his service in carrying messages to different parts of the field.

I am Colonel, very respectfully, your obedient servant.
John Buford
Brigadier General, Volunteers
List of documents with accompanying report.

A. Brigadier General Buford's report.
B. Recapitulation of losses.
C. List of casualties by name, rank, regiment, etc.
D. Reports of Reserve Brigade.
E Reports of Colonels Devin and Kellogg (1st Division).

Appendix J

100th anniversary celebration on Fleetwood Heights.
Photo from Culpeper Star Exponent

125th Anniversary Reenactment on Brandy Station battlefield.
Photo courtesy Tom Williams

**150th anniversary celebration on Fleetwood Heights.
Photo courtesy of Tom Williams**

CAVALRY CROSSING A FORD.

A LINE in long array where they wind betwixt green islands,

They take a serpentine course, their arms flash in the sun—hark to the musical clank,

Behold the silvery river, in it the splashing horses loitering stop to drink,

Behold the brown-faced men, each group, each person a picture, the negligent rest on the saddles,

Some emerge on the opposite bank, others are just entering the ford—while,

Scarlet and blue and snowy white,

The guidon flags flutter gayly in the wind.

Walt Whittman

Endnotes

[1] Confederate Conscription Act passed April 16, 1862
[2] Musick, 6th Virginia Cavalry, page 115
[3] McWhiney, Lee's Dispatches, pages 42 to 43
[4] McKinney, Brandy Station, Virginia, June 9, 1863: The Largest Cavalry Battle of the Civil War, page 53
[5] Hopkins, From Bull Run to Appomattox, page 126
[6] Musick, 6th Virginia Cavalry, page 36
[7] McDonald, The History of the Laurel Brigade, page 18
[8] McDonald, The History of the Laurel Brigade, page 20
[9] McDonald, The History of the Laurel Brigade, page 25
[10] Confederate Military History vol. 3, page 254
[11] Official Records, Series 1, Volume II
[12] Armstrong, 7th Virginia Cavalry
[13] Armstrong, 11th Virginia Cavalry, page 17
[14] 12th Virginia Cavalry, Frye, page 6
[15] Devine, 35th Battalion of Virginia Cavalry, page 2
[16] Devine, 35th Battalion of Virginia Cavalry, page 3
[17] Source: Confederate Military History, vol. IV, page 616
[18] Musick, 6th Virginia Cavalry, page 36
[19] Compiled service records
[20] Compiled service records
[21] 12th Virginia Cavalry, Frye, page 2
[22] McKinney, Brandy Station, Virginia, June 9, 1863: The Largest Cavalry Battle of the Civil War, page 53
[23] 12th Virginia Cavalry, Frye, page 15
[24] 12th Virginia Cavalry, Frye, page 16
[25] Devine, 35th Battalion of Virginia Cavalry, page 2

[26] Devine, 35th Battalion of Virginia Cavalry, page 11
[27] MCDP-1 "Force Planning and Organization" Pages 53-54
[28] MCDP 1-3 Achieving a Decision, Understanding the Situation page 25
[29] Coddington, The Gettysburg Campaign
[30] Armstrong. 11th Virginia Cavalry, page 40
[31] MCDP-1 Training Page 59/ MCDP 1-3 Critical vulnerabilities Page 30
[32] MCDP-1 professionalism page 56, MCDP-1 "Human Dimension" Pg 13, Speed and Focus MCDP-1 page 40, MCDP-1 "Complexity" page 7 "Uncertainty", MCDP 1-3 chapter 2 Achieving a decision Military Judgement page 24, chapter 4, Being faster.
[33] MCDP-1 professionalism page 56
[34] Speed and Focus MCDP-1 page 40
[35] MCDP-1 "Complexity" Page 13/ "Uncertainty" page 7
[36] MCDP 1-3 chapter 4, Being Faster
[37] MCDP-1 "Initiative and Response" Page 32 MCDP 3-1 Tactics, Cooperating/pages 91 to 98
[38] MCDP-1 Federal use of "combat Power" Page 39 MCDP 1-3 Tactics, Adapting / pages 81 to 88
[39] Marine Corps Doctrinal Publication 1-3 Tactics, addresses having "Flexibility" with a plan Page 84.
[40] McKinney, Brandy Station, Virginia, June 9, 1863: The Largest Cavalry Battle of the Civil War, page 247

Select Bibliography

Books, Manuscripts and Manuals

Ballard, James Buchanan, *William Edmondson "Grumble" Jones, The Life of a Cantankerous Confederate*. Jefferson, North Carolina, 2017

Baylor, George, *Four Years in the Army of Northern Virginia*. B. F. Johnson, Richmond 1900

Beattie, Dan, *Brandy Station 1863: First step towards Gettysburg*, Osprey Publishing, Oxford, 2008

Blackford, W. W. Lt. Col., *War Years with JEB Stuart*, Charles Scribner's Sons, New York, 1945

Campaigning, MCDP 1-2, U.S. Marine Corps, Washington, D.C., August 1997

Carter, Robert G., U.S.A Ret. *Four Brothers in Blue or Sunshine and Shadows of the War of the Rebellion*. Austin, 1978

Crouch, Richard E., *Brandy Station: A Battle Like No Other*, Willow Bend Books, Westminster, MD, 2002

Coddington, Edward B., The Gettysburg Campaign: A Study in Command, Morningside Bookshop, Dayton, Ohio, 1979

Collins, Darrell L., *The Jones-Imboden Raid, The Confederate Attempt to Destroy the Baltimore and Ohio Railroad and Retake West Virginia*. McFarland & Company, Inc, Jefferson, North Carolina, and London, 2007

Confederate Military Manuscripts Series A: Holdings of the Virginia Historical Society

Crouch, Howard R. *Horse Equipment of the Civil War Era*. Fairfax, Virginia, 2003

Downey, Fairfax, *Clash of Cavalry: The Battle of Brandy Station*, New York: David McKay Company, 1959

Garnett, Theodore, Stanford, Captain, *Riding with Stuart*, White Mane Publishing Company Inc, Shippensburg, Pennsylvania, 1994

Grimsley, Daniel A. Major, *Battles in Culpeper County, Virginia 1861-1865*, Green Publishers, Orange, Virginia 1967

Hattaway, Herman and Jones, Archer, *How the North Won*, University of Illinois Press, Urbana and Chicago, Illinois, 1983

Hopkins, Luther W., *From Bull Run to Appomattox*. Baltimore, 1908

Intelligence, MCDP 2, U.S. Marine Corps, Washington, D.C., June 1997

Jackson, Thomas J. Letter to Colonel S. Bassett French, Caroline County, Virginia, 16 March 1863

Knopp, Ken R. *Confederate Saddles and Horse Equipment*. Orange, Virginia, 2001

Lambert, Dobbie Edward, *Grumble, The W. E. Jones Brigade 1863-64*, Wahiawa, Hawaii

Lee, Robert E., Capt., *Recollections and Letters of Robert E. Lee*, Konecky & Konecky, Old Saybrook, CT. 1904

Logistics, MCDP 4, U.S. Marine Corps, Washington, D.C., February 1997

Long, A.L., Brig. General, *Memoirs of Robert E. Lee: His Military and Personal History*, The Blue and Grey Press, Secaucus, New Jersey 1983

Longacre, Edward, *General John Buford: A Military Biography*, Combined Books, Inc, Conshohocken, PA. 1995

Marine Corps Operations, MCDP 1-0, U.S. Marine Corps, Washington, D.C., August 2011

McClellan, Henry B. Major, *I Rode with JEB Stuart: The Life and Campaigns of Major General J.E.B. Stuart*, Indian University Press, Bloomington, Indiana,1958

McDonald, William N. Captain, *A History of The Laurel Brigade*, 1907

McKinney, Joseph W., *Brandy Station, Virginia, June 9, 1863: The Largest Cavalry Battle of the Civil War*, McFarland & Company, Inc. and Publishers, Jefferson, North Carolina 2013

Miller, Keith, *Southern Horse*, Civil War Times, page 31, February 2005

Neese, George, M., Lt., *Three Years in the Confederate Horse Artillery: A Gunner in Chews Battery, Stuart Horse Artillery, Army of Northern Virginia*. The Neale Publishing Company, New York, and Washington, 1911

O'Neill, Robert F. Jr, Small but Important Riots: *The Cavalry Battles of Aldie, Middleburg, and Upperville June 10-27, 1863*, Privately Published 1993

Opie, John N., *A Rebel Cavalryman with Lee, Stuart, and Jackson*, W.B. Conkey Company, Chicago, Il. 1899

Planning, MCDP5, U.S. Marine Corps, Washington, D.C., July 1997

Strategy, MCDP 1-1, U.S. Marine Corps, Washington, D.C., November 1997

Tactics, MCDP 1-3, U.S. Marine Corps, Washington, D.C., July 1997

Thomas, Clarence, *General Turner Ashby, The Centaur of The South*, Eddie Press Corporation, 1907

Thomas, Emory M., *Bold Dragoon: The Life of J.E.B. Stuart*, Random House Inc., New York, 1986

Vandergrift, Donald and Webber, Stephen, *Mission Command: The Who, What, Where, When, and Why. An Anthology, Volume II*, Virginia, September 2018

Virginia Department of Confederate Military Records, 1859-1996 (subseries 2: Cavalry) Richmond, Virginia

Warfighting, MCDP 1, U.S. Marine Corps, Washington, D.C. 1989

Wittenberg, Eric J., *The Battle of Brandy Station*, The History Press, Charleston, SC. 2010

Idem and Davis, Daniel T., *Out Flew the Sabers: The Battle of Brandy Station June 9, 1863*, Savas Beatie, El Dorado Hills, California 2016

Newspapers

American and Commercial Advertiser, Baltimore, Maryland, June 11-12, 1863

Culpeper Star-Exponent, Culpeper, Virginia, June 10, 1963

Daily Examiner, Richmond Virginia June 9-13, 1863

Daily National Intelligencer, Washington, D.C, June 11-12, 1863

Daily Virginian, Lynchburg, Virginia, June 12-13, 1863

The Sentinel, Richmond, Virginia, June 11, 1863

The Whig, Richmond, Virginia, June 10-12, 1863

www.ingramcontent.com/pod-product-compliance
Lightning Source LLC
Chambersburg PA
CBHW071849230426
43671CB00012B/2114